A Note on the Cover Photo

The cover photo was taken in November 2007 by Ryan Lobo Photography (USA). It portrays the baptism of Joshua Blahyi in the ocean at Monrovia, the capital of Liberia, West Africa.

During Liberia's first civil war, Joshua Milton Blahyi was known as General Butt Naked. Because of his actions during the war that ravaged his country, an internet blogger once asked, 'Is this the most evil man who ever lived'? An edition of The Daily Mail Australia also ran an article on Joshua, with a heading titled, *The Most Evil Man in the World*.

It was the author's privilege and honour to baptize Joshua into Christ for the remission of his sins, and to receive the gift of the Holy Spirit.

Before his baptism, Joshua shared with Doug that as an 11-year-old boy, his tribal leaders made him their priest. He went on to reveal that even though he was just a boy, the tribe's spirit instructed him to offer child sacrifices. Joshua carried out the spirit's commands without hesitation. The 'boy' went on to lead a mercenary brigade and became known as one of the most inhumane and ruthless commanders in Africa's history!

 A catalogue record for this book is available from the National Library of Australia

Willis, Doug (author)
The Baptism of General Butt Naked, Africa's Notorious Warlord and Other Incredible Stories from the Life of an Australian Faith-Based Missionary Evangelist

ISBN 978-0-6485544-0-0
RELIGION / Christian Ministry / Missions
BIOGRAPHY & AUTOBIOGRAPHY / Religious

Typeset Whitman 11/16

Cover photo by Ryan Lobo Photography (USA)
Cover and book design by Green Hill Publishing

the BAPTISM *of* GENERAL BUTT NAKED

Africa's Notorious Warlord

AND OTHER INCREDIBLE STORIES
FROM THE LIFE OF AN AUSTRALIAN
FAITH-BASED MISSIONARY EVANGELIST

DOUG WILLIS

CONTENTS

2004—Doug with his family (L to R) Peter,
Philip, Doug, John, Deanne, Mark

Dedication

This book is dedicated to God and to the Lord Jesus Christ; to my late wife, Joyce; my children: Mark, Deanne, John, Peter and Philip; and to those whose faith may be wavering, and who just need a little 'faith-lift'!

ACKNOWLEDGEMENTS

I wish to acknowledge the loving support and valuable assistance of my wife, Loma, in the preparation of this book and for her unceasing encouragement for me to put pen to paper.

Special thanks also to my sons Mark and Peter and my friend Kerri Hibberd for their significant support in proofing my manuscript and to the family members who have helped finance the publishing and printing of this book.

Because I am primarily an evangelist, a preacher and teacher of the Bible, I have never considered myself a skilled writer, so the task has not been an easy one—which makes me very grateful for those who have helped me convey my thoughts and assisted me in presenting them to you.

FOREWORD

I am very pleased to be counted as one of Doug Willis' life-long friends. It was in the spring of 1960 that I first met this remarkable young Australian evangelist. At that time I was 32 and serving as the Minister of the Church of Christ in Catlin, Illinois. Doug Willis was just 26 years old!

Doug worked his way across the Pacific Ocean on a Norwegian freighter and then drove his way across America, arriving unannounced at Catlin. He introduced himself and I saw in this young man such inspiring impetus that I invited him to preach at the Catlin church the following Sunday morning. Doug inspired everyone with his Bible message and his Aussie accent. We were also a little bemused later that day when this young Aussie took off his shoes and socks and danced in the snow! Doug and I became instant friends and that friendship has grown stronger over the years.

Before leaving Catlin, Doug made a heartfelt appeal for me to travel to Australia to preach the gospel. I thanked him, but assured him that I could not accept his invitation. When he asked me why, I informed him that I simply could not afford to undertake such a journey. He simply smiled at me and replied, 'God will supply your need!'

His invitation lingered in my heart for the next five years! Finally, in April 1966, I was led by God to dedicate the remainder of my life to foreign missions and determined that Australia would be my first overseas ministry. I worked for a full year to earn the money to undertake the travel with my family. During that year of planning,

Doug was busy arranging preaching meetings all over Australia. It was the year 1967 and I can state, without hesitation, that my continued overseas missionary work and preaching has been the direct result of Doug's challenge to my heart on that day in 1960.

Doug Willis later joined White Fields Overseas Evangelism (WFOE) as one of our full-time volunteer evangelists. We then worked side-by-side all over the world as partners in soul-winning.

Doug has always been such an inspiration and personally challenges me, due to his Bible knowledge; his ability to proclaim the unsearchable riches of Christ; and for his fearless willingness to go where no others dare to go. Throughout his long ministry, Doug has willingly gone anywhere that the Lord has called him to serve!

I thank God that Doug has written this book and I pray that you will read it and in doing so, receive a faith-lift that will see you grow in Christ. All who are privileged to know Doug are blessed by his ministry.

Reggie Thomas
Evangelist
Founder and Director (WFOE)
Joplin, Missouri

PREFACE

The author has written this book as an anthology: a collection of distinct and significant events which testify to God's hand upon his 60 years of ministry. His purpose is to share his experiences as a faith-based missionary evangelist, and to testify to the transforming power of the gospel. The book will give testimony to the providence, protection and provision of God, which occurred on a daily basis in the writer's life.

Doug Willis believes the things that he has experienced are comparatively insignificant in the overall scheme of God's dealings with man and with what other servants of Christ have accomplished. Nevertheless, he shares his experiences in order to give undeniable evidence of God's divine power. By sharing these attributes of the heavenly Father, he hopes you will find the accounts a bolster to your faith and that a younger preacher will be encouraged to pick up the baton and continue the work of evangelizing 'the fields white unto harvest'.

Unquestionably, he is convinced that Jesus Christ, and only Christ, saved and transformed his life. He needs no other proof that God is real! So many events have occurred during his worldwide ministry, far more than he can recall or record in this book: Instances that can only be explained as the providence of almighty God, his loving heavenly Father.

The author has travelled throughout Australia and 40 different nations of the world, conducting crusades, preacher-training seminars, college lectures and personal evangelism. Irrefutably, his life of ministry has been made possible through God's provision of finances, given freely by many faithful supporters.

Those who know Doug are acquainted with his daily habit of repeating the words of Psalm 40:16, *'The Lord be magnified!'*

ABOUT THE AUTHOR

'For you see your calling, brethren, that not many wise according to the flesh, not many mighty, not many noble, are called. But God has chosen the foolish things of the world to put to shame the wise, and God has chosen the weak things of the world to put to shame the things which are mighty.'

1 Corinthians 1:26-27

The author, Doug Willis, was born in the year 1935 in Sydney, New South Wales. At the outbreak of WWII, when he was four years old, his family moved to the far-north coast of the state, where he grew up on their dairy farm at Tregeagle, just east of the city of Lismore.

In 1950, after breaking several athletic records and winning six out of seven events in a combined Far North Coast High School Carnival, to his surprise he was chosen outstanding athlete for the games. His youthful hopes and dreams were then set on the Olympic Games, which were scheduled to be held in Melbourne, Victoria, in 1956.

Sport occupied a large part of Doug's journey as a teenager: athletics, rowing and boxing frequently took him from Lismore to Brisbane, Queensland, as well as to many other places, to compete in state championships and against Australian champions.

The author's father acted as boxing coach for both Doug and his brother Ken. In 1927 their father, Wilbur Harry Willis, was the Australasian Amateur Featherweight Champion. His boxing prowess saw him selected as one of the champions to compete in the 1928 Olympic Games in Amsterdam, Netherlands. However, lack of funding for the Australian team saw this great honour and opportunity fall by the wayside.

Shortly after Doug won a middleweight boxing competition and survived an exhibition round with the then Australian Amateur Champion, Tony Madigan, his career in the ring came to an abrupt end. Madigan went on to win the Bronze Medal at the 1960 Olympics, having been defeated in the semi-final by Cassius Clay (Muhammad Ali).

For the author, the slim chance of being destined for glory on the sporting field simply faded into insignificance, for he had become aware of God's call on his life and the far greater glory of eternal reward.

Doug's father, Wilbur Harry Willis (1928 Olympian)

In late August 1951, Doug publicly confessed his faith in Christ and was baptized soon after at the Church of Christ in Lismore.

By this time his parents had moved to Bexhill, 10 kilometres north of Lismore, to a new property. On New Year's Day 1953, while home alone on the dairy farm, his life was completely turned around by God. The solitude of that day gave him the opportunity to do a lot of soul-searching, meditating, praying and reading of the Scriptures.

Shortly before this day, Doug had attended a youth camp at

Tallebudgera Creek on the Gold Coast, Queensland. The Scripture passage studied during the camp was James 4:4-5: *'Adulterers and adulteresses! Do you not know that friendship with the world is enmity with God? Whoever therefore wants to be a friend of the world makes himself an enemy of God. Or do you think that the Scripture says in vain, "The Spirit who dwells in us yearns jealously."'*

Doug's conscience was under deep conviction concerning his worldliness as he endeavoured to live out his Christian life.

Consequently, during that New Year's Day of 1953, one by one, God convicted him of the things in his life that were holding back his spiritual growth and not allowing the Holy Spirit to fill his life. He knew that in order for God to use him for His glory, he had to let go of some things that he held dear.

At the end of the day, Doug made a commitment to God to give up six things that he knew were hindering him from achieving his highest potential to serve Christ and to grow in grace and knowledge.

As night came, a peace filled his heart and the next day, joy and power enabled him to start witnessing to others. That same joy and power in sharing the gospel has constantly remained with Doug, as the Lord provides him with countless opportunities to preach the gospel and witness to God's saving power.

In 1954 he entered the Churches of Christ Bible College at Woolwich, Sydney and at the beginning of his final year in College he married Joyce Bulmer of Wingham, New South Wales.

In February 1958 Doug and Joyce, together with their six-week old son Mark, moved to Western Australia where he ministered at a church in the eastern wheat belt. Accepting this first full-time ministry was conditional on him being released by the church when invitations arose for him to conduct gospel crusades.

In 1960, after conducting one chapel and two tent missions in Western Australia, he was led by God to seek further experience in crusade evangelism by observing the ministries of several well-known American evangelists. He had no funds to pay for his fare or to undertake such an adventure, but in a very amazing way God opened the door for him to work his passage to America.

It was on this first trip to the United States that Doug met Reggie Thomas, a wonderful God-used evangelist. From that first meeting, a strong bond of friendship formed between the two men: a friendship that continues to this day, as they share together in world evangelism.

In December 2004, Joyce, Doug's devoted wife of almost 49 years was called home to glory! Following her death, he spent an extended time in international ministry: evangelizing, conducting training-seminars and preaching.

However, God had an ongoing plan and unexpected purpose for his life! In November 2006 a new chapter of his life's story opened when he married Loma Graydon, a widow and member of his hometown church in Lismore.

Each story of this book is intricately woven around a lifetime passion of seeking to win the lost to Christ. What makes these accounts more amazing is the fact that Doug's crusades, seminars and world tours were all paid for from unsolicited funds freely given by God's children.

In declining to receive a salary, God provided for Doug's family; for his ministry expenses and for his personal needs—for this reason many know him as a faith missionary. The events he shares exemplify faith-based living and bring to light Doug's amazing journey from 'cow bails to the court of a King'—a place so far removed from his home town where God first called him to preach the gospel.

Each page is filled with accounts of God's mighty acts of providence, protection and provision and the author prays that as you read, you will not marvel at what he has achieved, but give all glory to the King of kings and Lord of lords.

A brief autobiography of Doug's personal reflections on his life and years of ministry can be found in the final chapter of this book.

Loma J Willis OAM
Bachelor Degree in Bible Studies
(Christ's Evangelical Foundation)
Bachelor of Business & Professional Studies
(Southern Cross University)
Woody Point QLD

'Not that we are sufficient of ourselves to think of anything as being from ourselves, but our sufficiency is from God, who also made us sufficient as ministers of the new covenant, not of the letter but of the Spirit; for the letter kills, but the Spirit gives life.'
2 Corinthians 3:5-6

The author, Doug Willis (aged 26)

the stories

THE BAPTISM OF GENERAL BUTT NAKED

'Now, therefore,' says the LORD, "Turn to Me with all your heart, with fasting, with weeping, and with mourning." So rend your heart, and not your garments; return to the Lord your God, for He is gracious and merciful, slow to anger, and of great kindness; and He relents from doing harm. Who knows if He will turn and relent, and leave a blessing behind Him.'

Joel 2:12-14[a]

THIS AMAZING STORY SPEAKS profoundly of God's grace, forgiveness and purpose for each of His children.

My brother in Christ, Joshua Milton Blahyi, was formerly known during Liberia's first civil war as General Butt Naked. Because of his actions during the war that ravaged his country, an internet blogger once asked, 'Is this the most evil man who ever lived'? An edition of The Daily Mail Australia also ran an excellent article on Joshua, with a heading titled, *The Most Evil Man in the World.*

I first met Joshua in November 2007 while on an evangelistic trip to Monrovia. It was my privilege and honour to baptize this man into Christ for the remission of his sins and to receive the gift of the Holy Spirit.

In his autobiography *The Redemption of an African Warlord: The Joshua Blahyi Story,* Joshua relates many incredible encounters with his tribe's spirit. I feel privileged that he trusted me sufficiently to sit with me and personally reveal many of his life experiences.

Joshua shared that as an 11-year-old boy, his tribal leaders made him their priest. As Joshua continued to disclose his story to me, it quickly became clear that African tribes are very much under the control of Satan and that they are led by several rival spirits.

While still just a boy, the tribe's spirit instructed Joshua to offer child sacrifices. Joshua carried out the spirit's commands without hesitation! Some years later, at the beginning of the first of the nation's two civil wars, Joshua's services as an army general were very much in demand. And, once again his tribal spirit instructed him! This time he was told to go into battle naked, except for sneakers and his rifle, with the promise that if he did, he would be protected from the enemies' bullets.

Joshua and his soldiers (who were often boys in their early teens or younger) committed many atrocities and acts of violence during the civil war! The details and pictures of his war crimes can be viewed on the web.

As a warlord, he was greatly feared by the people. In this small nation, it is estimated that 250,000 people were killed during the first civil war. Of these, Joshua personally admitted to having killed some 20,000 victims. It is not surprising that he became known as one of the most inhumane and ruthless commanders in Africa's history.

After the first civil war came to an end, the Lord challenged a Christian man who was working in the nation, to go and witness to Joshua. At this time Joshua was still a man feared by the general population. Joshua told me that because of his infamy, he was amazed that someone would have sufficient courage to come and present the gospel to him.

Joshua also disclosed that God had given him a prior 'spiritual awakening' and that when this stranger knocked on his door, he was ready to listen and accept Christ as his Lord and Saviour. The Bible tells us, '*But as many as received Him, to them He gave the right to become children of God, to those who believe in His name: who were born, not of blood, nor of the will of the flesh, nor of the will of man, but of God*' (John 1:12-13).

As we sat and shared over a meal that day in the Hotel where we were both staying, it was not long before we became engaged in a deeper conversation about the gospel and salvation. We shared for more than an hour before he told me that he had never been baptized.

The following day we met once more, and after spending further time together in the Scriptures, Joshua asked me if I would baptize him. He said that the Scriptures I had shared with him the night before, from Matthew Chapter Seven, had really convicted him.

> 'Not everyone who says to Me, "Lord, Lord!" shall enter the kingdom of heaven, but he who does the will of My Father in heaven. Many will say to Me in that day, "Lord, Lord, have we not prophesied in Your name, cast out demons in Your name, and done many wonders in Your name?" And then I will declare to them, "I never knew you; depart from Me, you who practice lawlessness."'
>
> **Matthew 7:21-23**

Following Joshua's request, I contacted the local representative of WFOE and asked him if he would be prepared to come and help me baptize Joshua. On discovering 'who' I was going to baptize, my co-worker was very hesitant, but, finally he agreed to assist.

(This godly man, Eric Foday, has since gone home to glory! He became critically ill during the Ebola plague, when the hospitals were overcrowded with emergencies. His family took him to the hospital for medical help, but he was turned away, despite his urgent need for dialysis. An appeal for financial support went out internationally and funds were raised to cover the cost of a doctor going to Eric's home, but by the time the funds reached his family, it was too late to save his life).

Whilst making the arrangements for Joshua's baptism, a USA film crew approached me and asked if they could be present to film his immersion. Eric Strauss and Daniele Anastasion (Directors) were in the country filming a documentary on Joshua's life: *The Redemption of General Butt Naked.* The documentary won the 2011 Sundance Film Festival's Excellence in Cinematography Award. The Los Angeles Times wrote about the movie, 'A compelling portrait of an extraordinary complex personal odyssey that portrays both the power and the limitations of faith and forgiveness'.

More recently, Ryan Lobo, the Co-Producer and photographer for the documentary, presented a compelling dialogue on TED Talks, which includes a photo of the moment when Joshua is about to be baptised in obedience to His Lord and Saviour Jesus Christ.

When making the film, the crew travelled throughout Monrovia with Joshua, who was seeking forgiveness from the families and victims of his ruthless atrocities. Ryan recounts in his TED presentation that during this tour, he was personally confronted with the truth of real forgiveness—a forgiveness that he never thought possible.

The incredible change in Joshua's life can only be explained by the truth in the Scripture passage, '*Therefore, if anyone is in Christ, he is a new creation, old things have passed away, behold, all things have become new*' (2 Corinthians 5:17—GW). Instead of living for self and Satan, Joshua is now living for God. He has found a worthwhile purpose and calling for his life.

It was a glorious day as we headed down to the ocean for Joshua's baptism. When we came out of the water, we joined together in a circle with those who were there to witness the baptism and sang, 'I have decided to follow Jesus, no turning back, no turning back'. I shared with those present the words of Jesus: '*And Jesus said to him, "No one, having put his hand to the plow, and looking back, is fit for the kingdom of God"*' (Luke 9:62).

While we were singing, I phoned Loma in Australia to share the occasion and to let her hear the joy coming straight from our hearts as we stood together on the sandy shore. Joshua also spoke to her, telling of his great joy. Even though the call was in the early hours of her morning, when I arrived home Loma told me that the sound of the ocean waves rolling in and the voices lifted to God in praise was something that she would never forget!

My reply to her was that King David saw to it that those who remained behind from the battle to watch over their 'stuff' got to share in the spoils and trophies from the battle-field. For Loma, who for health reasons was unable to travel with me, this was her trophy to treasure.

In 2008, the former General Butt Naked confessed his crimes at Liberia's Truth and Reconciliation Commission (TRC). To the disbelief and anger of many who had been completely broken by his crimes, the TRC pardoned Joshua, because of his sincere admission of guilt and his genuine remorse for what he had done.

The TRC also commended Joshua for his candour in exposing child sacrifice and cannibalism in that nation. Because of the hostile reaction to the TRC's decision from many within the nation, Joshua fled the country and for a few years he was estranged from his family, hiding in Ghana, due to his fear of reprisals from his victims and their relatives.

Unlike all the other warlords who appeared before the Commission and openly boasted of their roles in the civil war, Joshua was the only warlord granted amnesty, due to his repentant behaviour and his plea for Liberians to forgive him for the atrocities he had committed.

In 2016 Joshua founded a rehabilitation farm on 52 hectares in Sinoe County. The project includes training young men who were once child soldiers and helping them recover from their past, which for some now includes drug addiction. Together they are producing their own mud bricks and building eco-friendly homes on the farm to help other young boys and girls get their lives back on track.

Today Joshua is President of the End Time Train Evangelistic Ministries. He is married and has four children. Joshua travels the nation of Liberia primarily as an evangelist, but also still seeking out those he once victimized, in search of forgiveness.

Surely the words of the prophet Micah are very fitting for Joshua: *'Who is a God like You, pardoning iniquity and passing over the transgression of the remnant of His heritage? He does not retain His anger forever, because He delights in mercy. He will again have compassion on us, and will subdue our iniquities. You will cast all our sins into the depths of the sea'* (Micah 7:18-19).

> *'For His anger is but for a moment, His favour is for life; weeping may endure for a night, but joy comes in the morning ... You have turned for me my mourning into dancing; You have put off my sackcloth and clothed me with gladness.'*
> **Psalm 30:5-11**

2007—Joshua's baptism in the ocean at Monrovia (Ryan Lobo Photography USA)

2007—Raised to walk in newness of life (Ryan Lobo Photography USA)

2007—And he went on his way rejoicing!

HITCHHIKING WITH THE GOSPEL

'And when He has come, He will convict the world of sin, and of righteousness, and of judgment: of sin, because they do not believe in Me; of righteousness, because I go to My Father and you see Me no more; of judgement because the ruler of this world is judged.'

John 16:8-11

IN MY YOUNGER PREACHING days, hitchhiking on highways in Australia was not considered dangerous.

During those years, my income from gifts totalled about half of what was considered an 'average' wage! By now, Joyce and I had four children and were a one-car family, living in a house on my father's dairy farm which was located 11 kilometres north of the city of Lismore. This may help to explain why I had to leave our car at home and hitchhike to my ministry destinations. As I travelled, I did not use the usual 'thumb a ride' sign, but instead would stand, pray and point in the direction that I was going.

Truckie Hears the Gospel

One day, as I was returning home from a crusade in Victoria, a truck driver offered me a ride. Once settled in a vehicle it was always my habit to find out the driver's need and, if possible, meet it! This strategy for personal evangelism was part of a motto that I carried inside my Bible for many years.

On this particular occasion, we travelled many miles discussing gospel facts and spiritual truths. Before the driver stopped to let me out of his truck, he said to me, 'You know, normally I would never have talked to a minister like this'!

I thank God for the wonderful opportunities He provided to me on so many occasions! People who normally would never have darkened the door of a church building heard the gospel during my many hitchhiking experiences.

Hitchhiking the Hume Highway

On another occasion, as I stood on a roadside outside a southern New South Wales town, a travelling salesman drove towards me, travelling at speed. I prayed and pointed in the direction I wanted to go, but, to my disappointment, he did not even slow down. However, much to my surprise, shortly after he appeared once more, having turned around and driven back to offer me a ride! Before long we were engaged in a spiritual conversation!

This man was very open to the gospel and the teachings of the Lord's church and he indicated that he wanted to hear as much as possible. Before finally leaving him that day, I provided him with the name of a contact at the Church of Christ in Albury, Victoria. As he was about to drive off, he told me a mind-blowing thing! He said, 'You know, I never pick up hitchhikers, but when I drove past you today, something inside me caused me to turn around and come back to pick you up. I just couldn't drive on'!

Hitchhiking the New England Highway

Once, while hitchhiking on the New England Highway in New South Wales, yet another travelling salesman offered me a ride and I soon discovered that he also was very interested in hearing the gospel message.

After he made a scheduled stop to take care of business in Glenn Innes, he changed his travel plans! Instead of staying the night in 'Glen', he drove on to his next stop, so that he could have more time to listen to the glorious message we call 'The Gospel'.

The Personal Worker's Motto

Shortly after becoming a Christian and before going to Bible College, I was reading a book on personal witnessing. The book titled, *Taking Men Alive* by Charles G Trumbull, identified that the biggest mistake one can make in personal evangelism is to 'say nothing'. I confess that there have been many times when I have not spoken up and there are still times that I make that same mistake. But, abundant blessings have always followed when I have practised Trumbull's advice.

Recorded in his book is a motto for personal workers which states: *'Whenever I have the opportunity to control the conversation, I will endeavour to discover the person's need, and if possible meet it'.*

The very first time that I applied this 'motto' I was hitchhiking! I was hardly seated in the car when the man who picked me up told me that he was leaving his wife. He went on to share that he was 'taking off' with just the few belongings that he had in the vehicle. I shared the gospel's life-changing power with him and I also shared the eternal consequences of rejecting Christ.

That day this man went out of his way and drove me all the way to my home, dropping me off at the end of the lane where I lived. He then stepped out of the car to shake my hand and say goodbye. At the time, I was a little mystified as to why he was visibly shaking!

The Holy Spirit's Convicting Power

Later in my ministry, I came to realise more fully the power of the gospel. Over the years, I have observed many such individuals who were convicted by the gospel in my crusade meetings. Some men's faces turned red! I was told that another man asked his friend, 'How did he know so much about me'? One man on leaving a meeting said to me, 'I got the message'. To this day, I do not know what he was talking about! He obviously thought I knew of some personal sin and that I was preaching the message that morning just for his benefit.

On another occasion, one young woman left the meeting very disturbed, vowing that she was never coming back. Two weeks later this same lady returned with her mother and at the close of the meeting both women accepted Christ as their Lord and Saviour.

It is truly written, *'The Holy Spirit will convict of sin, righteousness and judgement to come.'* Evangelists are simply the channel God uses—instruments in the Potter's hand.

'Knowing, therefore, the terror of the Lord, we persuade men; but we are well known to God, and I also trust are well known in your consciences.'

2 Corinthians 5:11

UNDER AIRPORT CONFINEMENT

'For the LORD will judge His people and have compassion on His servants, when He sees that their power is gone.'

Deuteronomy 32:36[a]

AS I PEN THESE incredible events, it is difficult for me to believe they actually took place—but they did!

During 1992, my preaching schedule took me to several West African nations. On one particular trip, I was to spend several days in French-speaking Cote d'Ivoire. At that time the Ivory Coast did not have an embassy in Australia. Therefore, I contacted the French Embassy to arrange my visa, but was informed that if I was staying for less than a week, which I was, no visa would be necessary.

A few days before leaving home, my elderly mother was admitted to the Southport Hospital on the Gold Coast for a gallbladder operation. Because of her age and pending surgery, I advised my contact in the Ivory Coast, Kouame Sylvestre Adjoumani, that my arrival could be delayed if things did not go well with her surgery.

On my arrival in Abidjan, the airport immigration officer advised me that the rules for entering the country had recently changed and that I now required an entry visa. At this point, the airport police took my passport and advised me that they would be confining me to the departure lounge. As they led me away, I was so thankful that they had not placed me in the lock-up room, which I noted in passing was omitting a very 'strong' odour.

In the meantime, Kouame had travelled down from the country by bus, caught a taxi from the city to the airport, and then waited until all the passengers had come through customs, immigration and security. When I did not appear, he left and returned to his home, thinking that I had delayed my journey due to my mother's surgery.

Once home, Kouame phoned Reggie Thomas in America to tell him that I had not arrived as planned and to ask if he knew anything concerning my whereabouts. Reggie immediately called my wife Joyce, to tell her that I had not arrived. She later explained to me, 'It was the middle of the night when I received the call and I was not able to do anything, so I just committed you to the Lord and went back to sleep'. We made a good team, both trusting God to protect us in all situations!

Because of the problem that had arisen with my visa, the airline company shared part of the responsibility of the error and provided me with a bed for my first night's accommodation. Nevertheless, the next day I was directed back to the departure lounge where the only place for me to lie down was on the floor! There was a little internal kiosk to purchase food, but its supplies were very limited and the items were very expensive.

As a faith-based missionary my funds were also very limited, so that night I decided to try and find a way to exit the airport to buy food and find a bed for the night. So, squaring my shoulders and looking the custom, immigration, security and police officers straight in the eye, one by one, I walked calmly through all four checkpoints, without being stopped or questioned. Amazing! But, this occurrence was just the beginning of all that took place during my five-day ordeal!

After finding an African 'resort' near the airport and checking-in, I was directed to a small hut about 50 metres from the office. Contrary to my usual practice, and something I had never done before, nor have ever done since, I signed in under a pseudo name!

A few hours after I settled in for the night, I heard the police arrive and I was called to the office. I started to make my way towards them, praying and thinking, 'I am in big trouble now'.

However, as I approached, the manager called out, 'Wrong person! Go back'! I watched as the police left and asked myself if this was a case of being *as wise as serpents and as harmless as doves*? Maybe, or maybe not!

After a good night's sleep, I went back to the airport and once more, without my passport, I did the 'almost impossible' thing. I walked into the departure lounge, past all the soldiers, police, customs, immigration and security checks, without being asked once to present my passport.

Remarkably, all this was happening in a country not far removed from civil war and during a period when security was paramount, especially at the airport.

That night, an airport ground attendant, one of two to whom I was witnessing, took pity on me and allowed me to stretch out on a lounge in the business departure area. The only problem was—she had to lock me in!

In order to buy affordable meals during my five-day detention, I repeated this process at least six times, as I walked unhindered in and out of the airport. On one occasion I took another Australian with me, who had also been given the same incorrect advice by the French Embassy in Australia. While we were eating in the outside restaurant, I noted that some police officers from the airport had come in to eat. One of them kept looking at me with what I thought was a bemused, or, perhaps a somewhat 'befuddled' smirk on his face.

One day, whilst filling in time in the departure lounge, I had the opportunity to share my circumstances with a French businessman who was waiting for his flight. Before he left, he gave me his wife's phone number and told me to call her to see if she could help. I contacted his wife, who reported back to me with the news that the British Embassy had told her they were unable to help. However, she had been told that the Canadian Embassy would contact the

Minister for Immigration on my behalf. The problem was that the Minister was not available on that day, because he was attending a football match.

I then gave this kind woman the name and address of my contact, Kouame. The exact size of the town where he lived is still not known to me, but I believe at that time it was between 15,000 and 20,000 people. My new found 'helper' told me later that when she called the Town Hall, she asked the clerk who answered the phone if he knew a man by the name of Kouame Sylvestre. The man hesitated for just a moment and then replied, 'Oh yes, he has just walked into the office!' She was then able to speak to Kouame and tell him that I was still at the airport.

I believe that we have to acknowledge that when events such as these happen over and over, it is a lot more than coincidence and much more like God's overruling action—He just didn't sign His name!

The next day Kouame once more took a bus ride down to the capital and caught a taxi to the airport, which was about 15 kilometres from the bus station.

The lady who had been my go-between called me again to tell me that he was on his way, so I went to the police desk and asked for my passport and went back and waited for Kouame in the departure lounge.

However, when he arrived, he went to the police desk and they told him that I had picked up my passport and left. So my friend, who by now was more than a little confused, caught a taxi back to the bus station to return once more to his home!

When he arrived at the bus station he realised he had left his ID card with the security police at the airport. So, yet again this faithful man of God turned around and headed back to the airport. In the meantime, I went again to the police desk, wondering why my contact had not arrived to collect me! They were very surprised to find that I was still in the airport and told me to go back to the departure lounge and wait.

This time, when Kouame arrived and went to the police desk to pick up his ID card, they escorted him to the departure lounge. When they found me, I was asleep in the *'peace that passes all understanding'*, the peace that only Christ can give! When they woke me, my heart filled with joy and gratitude to the God who watches over His servants.

But, I must share that there was still another remarkable God-directed event to take place.

I was now free to leave the airport with Kouame, but I wanted to go back inside the terminal to say goodbye to the two Muslim ground staff to whom I had been witnessing. On this occasion, for the first time in five days, the guards prevented me from entering the building before I showed them my passport, which, praise God, was now safely back in my possession!

Clearly, without God's intervention on all the previous occasions, I would not have been allowed to leave, or re-enter the airport. I leave you to attempt to explain these events, without acknowledging the hand of God at work!

'I called on the LORD in distress; the LORD answered me and set me in a broad place.'

Psalm 118:5

BARE CUPBOARD—EMPTY PURSE!

'Bind them continually upon your heart; tie them around your neck. When you roam, they will lead you; when you sleep, they will keep you; and when you awake, they will speak with you.'

Proverbs 6:21-22

IT WAS NOT LONG after my wife Joyce and I had made a decision to decline regular financial support and live on faith-gifts, that we were conducting an aerosphere (an air-inflated tent) crusade in Rosebud, Victoria. We were staying in a rented house with our then four children, our pianist, a personal worker and a young couple who were providing the special gospel items and leading the crusade singing.

During this time, Joyce came to me and told me that there was only enough food left in the cupboard for her to prepare one more meal. There was less than 'two shillings' (approximately 20 cents) in her purse—and about the same amount in the bank.

That very same day, when I went to check our mail, I found a letter with a cheque inside. With this unexpected gift, our financial needs for the remainder of the crusade were provided! What was amazing about this gift was that the letter had been posted to our previous address, and then forwarded on to us in Rosebud. We had only been staying at the new address for about 10 days. Even now, I have no idea how the two post offices involved knew where to forward the mail!

They say that God is never late, but always on time. This saying was truly borne out in the timing and receiving of this cheque.

Trusting God for All our Needs

On another occasion, when the Lord was testing our faith, we were living in a house at Bexhill. We were out of money and because Joyce was at a meeting, I was serving the 'last' meal to our children! It was mashed pumpkin and potatoes: but the meal was mostly made up of pumpkin. When the 'meal' was finished, the children asked, 'Is that all, Dad'? When I replied 'Yes', they hopped down from the table without a single complaint or comment and went happily about their activities, completely accepting our way of trusting God for all our needs.

On the morning following this financial crisis and my need to provide for my family, my set Bible reading for the day included Psalm 81:10, *'I am the LORD your God . . . open your mouth wide, and I will fill it.'* Immediately, the Holy Spirit gave me the assurance that God would meet our needs that very day. I left my prayer room, which was set up in the old disused pigsty on my father's farm, and quickly walked back to the house and told Joyce what I believed God was going to do for us, 'today'. I stated, *'If we open our mouth wide* (faith), *God will fill it'* (supply all our needs).

Later that day, when our mail arrived, I found a letter with a cheque inside from a brother living in Victoria. The cheque was the largest gift we had received up to that point in time. The letter had been posted some days before! This man had never given any financial support to us before, nor has he given any since!

Sheep for a Week

Once when returning home with my family from Mt Isa, Queensland, we stopped to check on a driver who was parked on the side of the road (watching out for others is something most people do on the outback roads of Australia).

The man was a local sheep farmer and he had set out to travel south to his daughter and her family. Before leaving home he had killed and dressed a sheep to take to them. Shortly after leaving home, he hit a kangaroo and damaged the front of his utility, making it unsafe to continue on his journey.

There was nothing we could do to assist the stranded man, other than follow him as he limped back to his farmhouse. We then continued on our journey and as we said goodbye, the farmer offered us the dressed sheep. I will never know whether it was in appreciation for our stopping to enquire after his welfare, or whether it was seeing five children in our car that prompted this kind offer, but we gladly accepted.

'And my God shall supply all your need according to His riches in glory by Christ Jesus.'

Philippians 4:19

CRUSADE ORGANIZER JAILED

'The angel of the Lord encamps all around those who fear Him, and delivers them.'

Psalm 34:7

MY FIRST TWO VISITS to Chad, central North Africa, took me across a barren, wind-swept desert road. During the rainy season, this route is almost past being called a 'road'. (As I think about my ministry in Chad, there are a number of happenings on my first two trips into this nation, which now blend into one in my memory).

On my first journey across the desert from Nigeria, through Cameroon to Chad, the trip was so appalling that I determined in future to find any kind of aeroplane that would take me on my next journey. Alas, on my second visit to Chad, I could not find any scheduled flights, so I faced that dreadful desert road once more!

It is hard to know where to begin to share this account, but the story is too God-directed to overlook!

My contact in Nigeria was the late Ayo Bamidele, a dear friend and co-evangelist. Ayo, a godly martyr, was imprisoned many times; beaten many times; persecuted often; and finally murdered for his faith in 2011.

According to our pre-arranged plan, Ayo had gone ahead to organise my crusades in this Muslim nation. However, while arranging the platform and putting up banners advertising the crusade, the local police arrested Ayo and put him in jail.

After almost a week they released him, because the officers had witnessed him praying fervently and unceasingly and they determined that he was a God-fearing man. Having gained his freedom, Ayo sent me a telegram advising me not to come to Chad, and informing me that he was returning to Nigeria. However, I never received his telegram!

After flying into a northern city of Nigeria, I located a fill-up taxi that was travelling to Chad. As was the practice with 'fill-ups', I had to sit in the cab and wait until the vehicle had a full load—it was only then that the driver would leave! As we journeyed, the car was sometimes on the road and at other times it wasn't; because heavy rain had created an impassable quagmire!

As we were nearing our destination, I saw a sign on the side of the road that said that we were entering Cameroon. Protesting firmly to the driver, I stated that my destination was Chad, not Cameroon!

'Oh', he said, 'We have to cross through Cameroon to get to Chad'.

'Well, OK', I gloomily thought to myself, 'but it would have been good if someone had told me this before we left, so that I could have obtained a visa to enter Cameroon'.

Arriving at the border crossing, the officers asked me for the usual bribe, which I did not have and most certainly did not want to give. Finally, they took my passport into the office and sometime later a tall Sudanese-looking African official came out and gave it back to me, with the visa stamped inside. This was a real surprise to me, for he did not ask for something in return. So with much delight and with a glowing smile I said, 'Thank you, very much'.

'Not at all' he replied, 'It is my duty'.

As I walked away, I could not help question in my mind if he was an angel in disguise!

Shortly after, I was on the back of a motorbike, with my suitcase precariously balanced between me and the rider and my backpack over my shoulder. We were following other taxi-bikes across narrow strips of hardened mud tracks to the next border crossing. On arrival, Ayo was not at the border to meet me, so I caught a bus into town and found the Summer Institute of Linguistics (SIL) compound, where the missionaries kindly provided me with accommodation in a room by the gate.

During the following days, the rain continued to pour down. Most of the roads in the capital of N'Djamena were not sealed and some of the mud brick houses were falling down as a result of the heavy rain. During this time I was able to get some much needed rest. I did not mind, because I was still recovering from a bout of malaria which I had contracted in Nigeria. I also went everywhere searching for Ayo!

On the last day before I would be forced to leave and return to Nigeria, I called at a Christian school, still looking for anyone who had knowledge, or had seen a Nigerian preacher by the name of Ayo.

Later that day a teacher from the school came to where I was staying and shared with me his inspirational testimony. He told me that when he was preparing to leave his family home, his father, who was a preacher, had left two things on the table in his bedroom: a bundle of money and a Bible. His father then told him to make a choice! Which would he take? He humbly shared with me that he chose the Bible!

After spending some time sharing and teaching the New Testament requirements for salvation and the practices of the New Testament church, this young man, Michael, said to me, 'I believe that God sent you to Chad just for me'.

'So do I', was my reply!

(It is encouraging for me to share that Michael, with the help of a few other co-workers, has since set up several New Testament churches in Chad).

Once back in Nigeria, I made my way to Ayo's home, all the time going over in my mind the things I was going to say in chastising him for not being at the border in Chad to meet me. It was only when sitting with Ayo at his home that I learnt of his ordeal with the police and the telegram I had missed. My thoughts immediately went to Michael and I asked myself was my trip in vain—or did God have a purpose for me going to Chad?

With God All Things Are Possible

On my second trip to Chad, once more in the aftermath of heavy rain and flooding, the 'fill-up taxi' I was travelling in got halfway across that unwelcoming desert road when the starter motor on the vehicle failed. Every time we stopped, we had to get out and push the vehicle to get it started. On one occasion, when I was helping to push the vehicle through the mud, I lost a sock, forever buried in the deep, sodden, tacky mud. I was thankful that I had removed my only pair of shoes before getting out of the car that day!

Then, just when I thought things could not be more serious, the vehicle's clutch burnt out, I suspect as a result of all the water we had travelled through. There was only one town located on this unforgiving route across the desert, and praise God, when the car finally quit, it was just outside that very town.

Even so, I was now stranded in the middle of the desert! I stood waiting while the Muslim passengers travelling with me went to their set time of prayer. I wondered what I should do! I did not want them to think I was not willing to pray, nor did I want to make a public show of my own praying. So I went around the bend, knelt down and prayed and as I did, God touched the sky with a majestically vibrant, perfect sunset. To me, this was another incontestable display of His watchfulness and nearness.

Miraculously, in this small wasteland town, the driver found another car, although it may not be correct to call it a 'car'! After much protesting on my part, we all paid the driver another fare for the replacement vehicle and we set out once more. We did not get very far that night, as the road was flooded and impassable. There was nothing else we could do but turn around and head back to that small desert town, where we found a shed with a heap of straw to bed down on for the rest of the night.

The next day, when we arrived at the Chad border, I was totally exhausted from having helped push both cars in the hot desert sun. I have no doubt that I must have looked rather odd, for I had placed a handkerchief (knotted at the four corners) over my head to try to protect myself from the sun. My hat, always part of my travelling necessities, had been left behind in Nigeria!

Because a visa for Chad could not be obtained in Nigeria, I arrived at the border without one. It was immediately obvious that the sergeant on the boom gate was well intoxicated and had no intention of listening to my reasoning about why I did not have a visa. He kept shouting at me, 'Go back to where you came from and get a visa'.

I kept replying, 'It is impossible. We are the only car that has managed to get through. There is no way I can go back'.

While the inebriated sergeant was attending to other people, I decided to go across to the customs and immigration officials and ask their permission to enter Chad. After a few attempts, my requests were still proving hopeless. What should I do? Michael had arranged for me to wait at the border, where he was to meet me and help me enter the country. But, because I was running a day late and, in fact, because it was now Sunday, Michael was out preaching at a new location, helping to set up another New Testament church.

So, standing against the wall of the official's office, I bowed my head and prayed. As I prayed, a plan flashed into my mind! I turned to the official and asked, 'If I give you my passport will you let me go and stay in town for the night and I will go to the Immigration Office tomorrow and get a visa'?

Much to my masked delight, he replied, 'Yes, that will be OK'.

Thankfully, I still had enough money to pay the small bus fare into town, but as a missionary living on faith-support, I did not have enough money to stay at a hotel. My lunch that day consisted of a solitary banana!

Because Michael was to have met me at the border on Saturday, I did not have an address to find him. On arrival, the bus driver put me down in the middle of town across from the city markets. I walked over to the first stall and asked the owner if he knew where the Church of Christ was located. I expected him to say, 'I have no idea'. In fact, that is exactly what he said, but, he also told me that there was a lad at the markets who was a member of 'that church'. He promptly called the lad over and asked him to take me to the address.

As the young man and his friend led me to my destination, I was reminded of the Bible story of a young Israeli maid and her faithful witness to her God. The young girl served in the house of Naaman, the Syrian general. The Bible tells us that the lass bore a faithful witness in a foreign land! It was obvious to me that this lad was also a faithful witness as he had clearly made it known in the midst of an antagonistic marketplace, in the middle of a Muslim city, that he was a Christian and a member of the Church of Christ.

As we walked down a number of streets, I thought to myself, 'This can't be true! He is probably taking me to the site of a Catholic church!' How wrong I was!

As we entered the gate of a compound, I saw Michael's wife and several church members in the courtyard. As I sat down, my eyes filled with tears. I was completely overcome with relief and emotion. I thanked God and marvelled at His goodness and providence. Shortly after, as messages went out to call the members back to the church at Michael's house, I shared in the Breaking of Bread with these beautiful disciples.

The Bible tells us that God 'flew on angel's wings'! That is the best way I can describe these two trips that were undertaken in order to proclaim the gospel in a hostile land and fulfil God's purpose for my ministry. I believe God carried me 'on the wings of an angel' during the ordeals I experienced!

> *'You have caused men to ride over our heads; we went through fire and through water; but You brought us out to rich fulfilment.'*
>
> **Psalm 66:12**

Travelling on the 'best side' of the road in Africa

2013—Doug with the late Ayo Bamidele's widow and family

QUEUED UP–CASHED OUT!

'As for me, being on the way, the Lord led me.'

Genesis 24:27[b]

AS A FAITH-SUPPORTED EVANGELIST, I was often challenged to leave home trusting in the Lord to provide for my family. My faith was, and always is, based on the word of God as found in Matthew 6:33, *'But seek first the kingdom of God and His righteousness, and all these things shall be added to you.'*

On one occasion in 1965, when we were very low on finances and food, God challenged me to go south-west to preach the gospel. But, what should I do about my family's needs? As a husband and a father, I knew it was my responsibility to take care of my family, as set out in 1 Timothy 5:8, *'But if anyone does not provide for his own, and especially for those of his household, he has denied the faith and is worse than an unbeliever.'* I took this Biblical direction very seriously, but I knew that it was also my responsibility to obey my Lord, by trusting Him to meet my needs. So, with a small amount of faith, I set out on the New England Highway. On my first night away from home I was able to stay with a godly family. Over the years, many such followers of Christ told me that their front door would always be open to me.

That night when I retired, there under my pillow was a £50 note! In those days, fifty pounds went a long way! What rejoicing, as this gift was sent back home, knowing that my family's needs were now met during my absence.

Faith and Integrity

On another occasion, when I was on a mission trip in India, I arrived at the airport in Chennai, to learn that my flight south to Kerala had left early that morning. The plane had departed without any of its booked passengers. I can only assume that the flight was taken over by VIPs or politicians. We were never given a reason! On arrival at the check-in counter, the attendant told us all that we would have to pay another fare for a new flight and because I was a foreigner, I would be required to pay US$50.

What could I do? I did not have any extra money to pay the additional airfare, nor did I hold any US dollars. I prayed and reminded myself that if it was true that all things are possible to those who believe, then I had to exercise that faith.

So, I waited in the queue with the rest of the passengers, waiting to see what God would do! I will admit that a little trepidation entered my mind as I waited in line, due to the fact that I needed to keep to my travel schedule. Meeting my set preaching agenda is something I have always made every effort to do. Over so many years, to my knowledge, there were only three occasions out of the many hundreds of appointments made for me, that I was not able to keep.

As I stood in line, I felt that not only my faith, but my integrity was also 'on the line', but I spoke to no one about my predicament, except God! Then, just before my turn came to go forward, an Indian businessman who was standing behind me in the queue reached over my shoulder and gave me a US$50 bill. He said to me, 'I have just returned from America and I have no need for this money'. I gratefully accepted the money and purchased my new ticket, but not before giving thanks to God and getting the address of this kind man. On arriving home to Australia I posted him a plush toy koala as a token of my appreciation for his kindness.

'Though the fig tree may not blossom, nor fruit be on the vines; though the labour of the olive may fail, and the fields yield no food; though the flock may be cut off from the fold, and there be no herd in the stalls—yet I will rejoice in the LORD, I will joy in the God of my salvation.'

Habakkuk 3:17-18

A FAMILY LIKENESS

'Do we begin again to commend ourselves? Or do we need, as some others, epistles of commendation to you or letters of commendation from you? You are our epistle written in our hearts, known and read by all men.'

2 Corinthians 3:1-2

ANOTHER REMINDER OF GOD'S providence was the day in 1960 when I arrived at Victoria Island, Canada, at the end of my long sea voyage from Western Australia. I had worked my way as a deck hand to North America on the *Kristen Bakke*, a Norwegian freighter, to gain experience from observing the American evangelists who were conducting crusades.

On leaving the ship, I went into a shop in Victoria, the capital of British Columbia. While the shop attendant was serving another customer, I looked around the store to buy a gift for my daughter, Deanne. When I went to the counter to pay, the woman serving said, 'I hope you don't mind me asking, but are you a Christian?'

When I replied 'Yes', she said that there was something about me that gave her an inner-sense that I too belonged to the same Lord as she did. Now, one must remember that I had been at sea for six weeks and probably looked more like any other rough Norwegian seaman, rather than a preacher. I was now some 18,000 kilometers from my home in Western Australia. It is only through the Holy Spirit who dwells in God's children, that such an observation is possible! Could this not be an extension of what we read in Romans 8:16, *'The Spirit Himself bears witness with our spirit that we are children of God.'*

Timely Reminders

A similar experience occurred on my last tour of Nigeria. After concluding the crusade, my co-workers and I stopped on the way back to our home base to enjoy a snack in a small fast-food shop. We ordered our 'delights', but before I could pay, a Nigerian man sitting at a table nearby stood up, and walking toward me, he insisted on paying my bill. As he handed me the money he said, 'Something tells me that you are a man of God and I should pay for your food'.

In 2015 another occasion brought this passage of Scripture to mind! Whilst taking a short break on our way to Canberra, the nation's capital, my wife Loma and I stopped at the Hunter Valley Gardens in New South Wales. After viewing the magnificent flora within the gardens we went to the café to eat and, as always, prayed before we commenced our meal. We were in the café for quite some time and as we got up to leave, a lady sitting at another table with her family stopped us and said, 'Excuse me, but can I ask if you are Christians?' Had she seen us pray? We do not know, but there was clearly something about our persona that led her to engage in conversation with us that day. It was for us a timely reminder that we need to be ready, in season and out of season, to be a good witness for God and to share our faith!

> *'In this the children of God and the children of the devil are manifest: Whoever does not practice righteousness is not of God, nor is he who does not love his brother.'*
>
> **1 John 3:10**

GOD TESTS OUR FAITH

*'Do not fear; for God has come to test you, and that His fear
may be before you, so that you may not sin . . . To humble you
and test you, to know what was in your heart, whether you would
keep His commandments or not . . . That He might humble you
and that He might test you, to do you good in the end.'*
Exodus 20:20[b]; Deuteronomy 8:2[b]; Deuteronomy 8:16[b]

WHILE JOYCE AND I were living in Charters Towers, Queensland, I was ministering with Churches of Christ Home Missions, serving the isolated members and outback churches in the far north and north-west of the state. At the time, we were enjoying a period of financial stability! However, there was no room for complacency, because I had come to understand that these times of 'plenty' often happened before periods of real testing.

During this time I left home for a mission trip, forgetting to take my wallet. I realized my mistake after travelling about 15 kilometers from home. I stopped the vehicle and sat on the side of the road for some time, sort of arguing with the Lord, who was challenging me to 'go on in faith'.

What a test! I had no concern about accommodation, because my bed was set-up in the back of my vehicle, a Ford F100. The truck also had an extra fuel tank, but the extra tank still did not contain enough fuel for the vast expanse of north Queensland. I knew I would not have enough petrol to travel the distance planned for my mission itinerary.

Despite my human logic and reasoning, I accepted the divine challenge God placed on my heart and drove on to my first appointment. That evening at the close of the Bible study, my host, with a rather sheepish look on his face, poked a cheque into my shirt pocket. I was so thankful, yet a little surprised, because this man had never given me any financial support on previous visits, nor has he since! My surprise was not that God had answered my prayer, but that he had answered my prayer through this particular man.

Next morning I cashed the cheque, filled the F100 with petrol and continued on my journey!

It was early evening before I arrived at the property of a family whose name had been given to me by someone who wanted me to share the gospel with them. That night I asked, and was given permission to say grace before the evening meal. The next morning, knowing that I did not have enough petrol to get back home, I was once more facing a dilemma! I had made a commitment to God not to ask or tell anyone of my needs, except Him.

(When I was travelling in south-east Queensland conducting crusades, I would often call on a follower of Christ who lived on a farm outside Aratula. Every time I called to visit this godly man, he would take my truck over to his on-site petrol tank and fill my vehicle with fuel).

Fully aware that it is the practice of most farmers to have a small petrol holding tank on their properties, I asked God to help me with a plan! This led me to ask my host if I could buy some fuel, knowing that I did not have any money to pay for it, but with the intention of forwarding him a cheque once I arrived back home! When I asked about the fuel, he took my truck over to the farm tank and filled the F100 to the brim. When he came back, I asked about payment, but he refused to take any money! Truly, God is a faithful prayer-answering God!

Faith Rewarded

During this period of ministry I received a gift of US$30,000 from a brother in southern California. The funds were given for the work in India and were used to support many national evangelists, allowing them to preach the gospel to untold multitudes of people who lived in hundreds of unreached villages.

More recently, in 2015, another faithful brother from America sent me a gift of US$10,000! With these funds, we were able to send relief to several ministries that had been affected by the 'one in a century' flood in Chennai, India.

Neither of these gifts had been personally requested by me, but God has always supplied all of our needs through His people. I have always conducted my ministry on the Biblical example set by the apostle Paul and the evangelists working with the apostle John, who refused to take money from non-Christians.

During my many gospel evangelistic meetings, because unsaved people are encouraged to attend, it has always been my decision to never take up an offering to cover the crusade expenses, or my own personal needs. The gospel is freely received and freely given!

One such aerosphere crusade was conducted in a small church in western Sydney. In a pre-crusade planning meeting, the church treasurer became very agitated when he was told that we did not take up offerings as part of our nightly evangelistic meetings. I am so thankful that his strong objections were overruled by the elders that night! It could be said that it was somewhat ironic that this same brother was the person whose task it was to count the money from the one thanksgiving offering that we received on the last Lord's Day morning of the Crusade. When he counted the offering, the amount that had been given was almost exactly the amount needed to cover the crusade expenses! That day he rejoiced with us all and I suspect he never again doubted the need to work by the principles God has given us in His word.

'The young lions lack and suffer hunger; but those who seek the LORD shall not lack any good thing.'

Psalm 34:10

UNABLE TO LEAVE UGANDA

'But Jesus looked at them and said, "With men it is impossible, but not with God; for with God all things are possible."'

Mark 10:27

ON ONE OF MY several ministry trips into Uganda, East Africa, everyone entering the country was required to exchange US$1,000 for local currency with the government bank. On this particular journey, I was carrying money which had been given to me to provide help for the Christian widows, who were in great need. It was anticipated that with the gifted funds, the widows of the church could be set up in a self-supporting chicken business. So many in the nation were in great need! Following the genocide perpetrated by Idi Amin Dada, there were an estimated 3,000,000 widows in Uganda.

When I arrived at Entebbe International Airport, I read a sign that set out the Government's ruling in regard to local currency, but I did not realize that it was an absolute require-ment. I assumed it was simply a suggestion, or at the very best, an optional request. Certainly not a dictate! Perhaps my judgement was clouded by my wish to see that the widows received *all* of the funds that I was taking into the country, not just an amount that would be substantially depleted by the government's mandatory directive.

At the end of my tour, in the company of my co-worker, Jehoshaphat Kakooza, I left Kampala and made the 20 kilometer trip back to Entebbe Airport. It was only on our arrival, that I was informed that my plane was still on the ground in Athens, some five hours' flying time away.

While waiting for my flight, and because I had not exchanged any money at the government bank, I spoke to the head customs' offi-cial and asked if I would be able to leave without the bank receipt.

His answer was a very firm, 'No, sir, there is no way you can leave the country without the transaction receipt'.

Because of the delay in my flight departure time, Jehoshaphat and I decided to go back into the city and ask the relevant government minister if he would grant me special permission to leave Uganda without the imposed receipt. It was my hope that by explaining to him why I had exchanged my money at a private bank that provided better exchange rates and fees, he might grant me permission to leave. But no such luck! The minister was just as adamant in his response to me as the customs' official at the airport.

Feeling more than a little disheartened, we found a place to eat and pray, seeking God's will. We then devised a plan! Jehoshaphat was to wait on the viewing platform of the terminal and if he didn't see me board the plane, then he was to come back inside and get me. As we shared, we recalled the words of our Lord, *'If you can believe, all things are possible to him who believes'* (Mark 9:23). So we claimed His promise!

Because we had been held up in the city waiting for a fill-up taxi, we were late getting back to the airport. By the time I arrived at the check-in counter, there was only one other passenger standing in line. When the staff member handling my bags saw my Australian tag, he smiled and told me that he knew the (then) Australian Prime Minister, Bob Hawke. His interaction with me appeared to distract the other officials and apart from the anticipated question I had come to expect when going through the border of developing nations: 'What have you got for me today?', I found myself inside the terminal.

'Am I through, and on my way home' I asked myself? Not so soon! I noticed that near a far wall of the building there was a desk with a line of passengers waiting to have their documents checked. 'Surely', I assumed, 'this must be the place where they will ask for the receipt'.

In silent prayer, I finally arrived at the front of the line, where my passport was stamped, with no questions asked! I boarded the plane with a grateful heart and a cheerful wave to Jehoshaphat, who was standing, waiting and watching from the terminal observation platform.

'Not possible,' said the man in charge of airport customs! But, the ruler of all nations said, *'There are some things that people cannot do, but God can do anything'* (Mark 10:27[b]—CEV).

> *'For the weapons of our warfare are not carnal but mighty in God for pulling down strongholds.'*
> **2 Corinthians 10:4**

Preparing new converts for baptism in Nigeria

NEAR DEATH EXPERIENCES

'Be merciful to me, O God, be merciful to me! For my soul trusts in You; and in the shadow of Your wings I will make my refuge, until these calamities have passed by.'

Psalm 57:1

Spear Fishing in Western Australia

MY FIRST NEAR-DEATH EXPERIENCE took place in Busselton, Western Australia where I was conducting a tent crusade! One day, with a little time to spare, I decided together with fellow evangelist John Timms, to take a short break and go spear fishing off the end of the Busselton pier.

Before long, both John and I caught a couple of Dusky Morwong. These beautiful, colourful fish grow to a metre long and we were thrilled with our catch! The water was very pleasant and with some time still available, we continued snorkelling and free-diving. We were young, healthy and adventurous. Perhaps a little too adventurous, as we kept diving deeper and deeper! If the truth is known, John and I were trying to outdo each other; such was our friendship, which often saw us engaging in some form of competitive activity.

While reflecting on this experience recently and searching the internet, I found that the very location where we caught the fish was listed on the Busselton Tourism website and the information provided there confirmed my recollection of the location and the size of our catch. The dimensions of the Dusky Morwong we caught that day was not an exaggeration, as can so often be the case when recounting one's favourite 'fishing story!'

Diving deeper, I was aware that the oxygen in my lungs was getting very low. Then, I started admiring the magnificent coral on the pier posts. So stunning was the sight that I was 'lost' in the beauty of the moment. However, I realized my thoughts had changed from simple admiration, and I was now 'floating timelessly' with compelling thoughts of how good it would be to just 'stay' where I was!

At that moment, I was quickly jolted back to reality and I knew that something was very wrong! I was in danger of shallow water blackout (SWB), a real threat for those who push the boundaries too far when spearfishing. I needed to get to the surface before my oxygen was totally depleted. As I climbed onto the Busselton pier that day, I could do nothing more than thank God that I had made it back safely.

Starvation Diet in Guyana

In 1986, during my three months of evangelistic ministry in Guyana, South America, I found it conscientiously hard to adjust to seeing the people of that nation suffering from a lack of almost everything. The country's economy was in shambles and the nation was trying to survive on a North Korean style of communism.

All the daily comforts that I enjoyed in Australia were absent in this harsh country and my heart grieved for the local brethren. A shortage of fuel created a crisis for the taxi drivers, who had to line up at night, sleeping in their cars to be assured of getting petrol when the pumps opened at 3.00 pm the following day.

The flow-on of the fuel crisis created heavily overcrowded taxis, so it was not unusual for me to be riding in an old dilapidated Austin car (or similar), with up to 11 other passengers.

On one occasion, whilst sitting under a pile of odorous bodies, a policeman pulled our driver over and asked him to unload 'one' passenger. The driver politely obliged, then, when we travelled around the next corner out of sight of the officer, he simply picked up two more passengers!

Half way through this particular trip to Guyana, Joyce had been forced to return to America for medical treatment. Due to the environment we had been living in, we had both contracted scabies and there was no medicine available to us, not even at the hospital. I was on the mend, so, thankfully, was able to stay on for the remainder of my scheduled preaching itinerary.

After Joyce left, I was able to get accommodation in a boarding house. I decided that for me to be able to identify with the locals and appreciate their living conditions, I would halve my once-a-day meal of rice. At night my ration was one banana!

(Incidentally, if you like bananas, go to Guyana, for they grow every known variety on the planet! To survive 'eating boredom', I decided that I would try a different variety of the fruit every day).

My ministry schedule was physically challenging! I was preaching every night, conducting preacher-training seminars in the mornings and visiting contacts and church members in the afternoons.

It took some two weeks before I realized that my energy levels had dropped considerably. More worrying, I no longer wanted to eat at all. I knew that I needed to be eating more to combat my depleted energy. But how, when I was no longer motivated to eat! As hard as it was, I knew that I had to be eating sufficient food each day to survive.

I was now bordering on Anorexia Nervosa, but, with prayer and God's help, I was soon back to a normal eating plan and was able to continue for another six weeks of evangelistic ministry in this Caribbean nation.

Struck Down with Malaria

My first experience with malaria was in Zimbabwe!

Nobody noticed my absence from the team when the anti-malaria tablets were handed out and I was not aware that they were needed, or being provided. This oversight resulted in me contracting a serious bout of malaria, double pneumonia and the need to rest for several days.

My second attack of this life-threatening disease was while I was in Nigeria. I was told that the danger is not so much from malaria, but from the complications that often set in when a patient succumbs to the disease.

My schedule had taken me to Chad. Some helpful missionaries dosed me with medication and during the first week in the country I was able to rest, because I did not have any speaking commitments, due to the fact that my co-worker, the late Ayo Bamidele, was once more being held in jail.

On my third attack (once more in Nigeria) I became very ill and was taken to hospital, where blood tests confirmed that I did have malaria. However, I took one look at the condition of the hospital ward that day and for some reason, immediately felt just 'a little' better.

On this occasion, much against my wishes, one preaching commitment needed to be cancelled, but after a day and a night praying and fighting the disease, God placed me back on my feet so that I could continue with my planned meetings. I will never forget that night and day of prayer, the fever and the pain, but most of all, the blessing of God's healing hand upon me!

My fourth attack also began in Nigeria, just before leaving to return home to Australia. It was only after I had been home a week that I was once more diagnosed with the disease.

At this time, it was necessary for me to travel with my parents to Moree in north-western New South Wales to visit my sister Doreen, who had recently lost her husband to cancer. By now I was feeling very unwell, so I went to the medical clinic and the doctor immediately admitted me to hospital, where I stayed for the next 10 days. The medical team was very concerned about how sick I was and the doctor was having difficulty in diagnosing the particular strain of malaria.

Finally, it was decided to send my blood samples to the Tropical Disease Laboratory in Sydney for analysis. My doctor, Peter Whitnall (a Christian man who had grown up in the Church of Christ in Kingaroy) owned a light aircraft, which he used regularly to transport medical supplies from Sydney to Moree. When the laboratory contacted him with my results, Peter rang his pilot and asked him to wait at the Bankstown airport until a supply of quinine was delivered to him, so it could be brought back to Moree to commence my treatment.

At this point, some five days into my stay in hospital, I became gravely ill. I was extremely weak and unable to face food. Joyce and two of my children arrived, having been called to my bedside. But, praise be to God, after the arrival of the quinine and another five days of treatment, I was reluctantly released by Peter to be driven home to Lismore, which was some seven hours away.

I was so weak, the trip home almost didn't happen. But amazingly at each stage of the journey, by God's wonderful grace and care, I began to feel better and on arrival home I felt 'completely well' and gratefully spent time praising God.

All is Well—By God's Grace!

While driving my family to Tamworth in the New England region of northern New South Wales, a truck with a mechanical turning hand, pulled to the left to give the driver room to turn into a small road on his right hand side. The mechanical hand was barely visible to me, because it was mostly obscured by a load of timber the vehicle was carrying.

I was still travelling quite fast, for there were only a few vehicles on the road that day and the motorway was open and straight. I started to overtake the truck, thinking that he was pulling over to stop on the left-hand side of the road, but when I was almost level with the vehicle, the driver pulled across in front of me and started to turn to his right, into the side road.

A moment of real panic, as it seemed that there was nowhere for me to go!

With little time to think and far too late to brake, I prayed to God—and to avoid a collision I turned the car in the same direction as the truck was turning. It was all over in a flash and I found myself up a bank on the right-hand side of the road. As we came to an unceremonious stop, I got out, expecting to see some damage to the vehicle. I could hardly believe my eyes, for there were no obstacles on the bank where I had stopped and praise God, no damage to the car or its occupants.

There have been so many other close calls over the years, some seen and some unseen, when, but for God's protecting hand, a bad accident or death would have occurred.

'The LORD will strengthen him on his bed of illness; You will sustain him on his sickbed.'

Psalm 41:3

CHAD'S UNTOUCHABLES STRIKE

'Do not be afraid of sudden terror, nor of trouble from the wicked when it comes; for the LORD will be your confidence, and will keep your foot from being caught.'

Proverbs 3:25-26

IN 2006 GOD ONCE more opened the way for me to revisit the churches in Chad. My purpose was to conduct training seminars for the leaders; preach the gospel; and encourage the saints.

Having conducted a seminar and open-air gospel meetings in the capital N'Djamena, plans had been made by my co-worker for us to travel to another city, which was located some distance away. We set out on the trip in a heavily overloaded vehicle, and it wasn't long before the car broke down. As we waited on the side of the road for the vehicle to be repaired, I was given the opportunity to witness to several bystanders.

It was late in the evening by the time the car was ready to continue the journey. We set out once more, arriving at our drop-off point around 1.30 the next morning! We then needed to hire three motorbike taxis to take us to the home of our host. I was the pillion rider on the third bike! I sat clinging tightly to my luggage, which was placed hazardously between the rider and me. The road was a mix of dirt and gravel and full of very large ditches, so I was thankful that we were not travelling fast.

The first two bikes were bigger and travelling faster than we were and after a short time we lost sight of them. Next thing, out of the darkness dashed a ghostly figure and I found myself flying through the air onto the ground! As we approached him, he had lunged out and knocked the bike over. The 'ghostly figure' was a national security guard (soldier) who belonged to what the locals called *The Untouchables*.

Shaken, exhausted and in a state of shock, I picked myself up off the road to discover that my only injury was gravel rash. The rider, however, was bleeding from a nasty gash on his leg from where the motorbike had fallen on him. I discovered later that *The Untouchables* are never questioned about their actions, their many crimes, nor their callous treatment of the local populace.

As we struggled to our feet, the soldier, who was carrying a rifle over his shoulder, approached me and demanded that I give him my passport. Given that he wore the uniform and he was carrying the rifle, I thought it best to do as he requested! But as he walked away, I pleaded with him to return my passport.

Praying for some compassion from this militant, I called out in my best 'attempt' at French, 'Merci, merci', thinking I was crying, 'Please, please'—and not realizing until some years later that my poor grasp of the language meant just that—it was an 'attempt'—for I was actually calling out, 'Thank you, thank you'.

Mercifully, he turned around, came back and handed me my passport, but, as he did so, he snatched my mobile phone from my belt and once more became a ghostly figure, as he ran back into the darkness.

When we finally arrived at the house in the village where we were to spend the night, I shared with those present what had happened. Our host told us that such attacks happened regularly and he added that he believed God's hand had been upon us, for *The Untouchables* usually shot their victims, so there would be no witnesses to their crimes! After I stopped shaking, I did manage to get a little sleep on a makeshift bed.

Next morning we reported the incident to the local military headquarters, but, because of what we had been told about past atrocities by these corrupt soldiers, we were not expecting anything more to come of it!

Nonetheless, a few days later, after returning from various village gospel meetings, we called back to the military base to see if anything had happened as a result of our report. To our amazement, they told us that the motorbike rider had identified the soldier responsible for the attack and that his superiors had apprehended and detained him.

At that point the soldier was brought out to face us! After my co-worker, Michael, presented the gospel to the soldier (as well as to everyone else in the room), he proceeded to give the perpetrator a good 'dressing down'!

Then I stood and faced him and asked, 'I need to know! Why did you run? You were carrying the rifle'.

He replied, 'Because of the fear of God'.

The army officer in charge then told me that the soldier had already sold my phone, so I never saw it again! However, I was thankful that God had protected me, so that I could continue to serve Him, and that in this time of great testing, I could still strive to save others.

At the time that the incident happened, there was only one independent radio station in Chad. We approached the station and told them our story and they asked if I would be willing to be interviewed, in order to relay to the public what had happened in the attack. The station manager said he believed that the outcome of our encounter would be of immense encouragement to the local people.

He added that if they could hear and comprehend that they could take a stand against *The Untouchables*, it would also give them hope. Hence, my interview took place, but to assure my protection, the radio station waited until I left the country before broadcasting the interview.

My strength was in the knowledge that regardless of the dangers, we must be ready in season and out of season to preach the word.

'Many are the afflictions of the righteous, but the LORD delivers him out of them all.'

Psalm 34:19

AMAZING CONNECTIONS

'A man's heart plans his way, but the LORD directs his steps.'
Proverbs 16:9

DURING MY LONG YEARS of ministry I have experienced many extraordinary, God-given connections that literally changed the course of my life's work.

My decision to work my passage to America on a Norwegian freighter came to fruition because I was convicted in my heart of God's initial, clear calling on my life. That 'calling' was to tell lost souls how to be saved by fulfilling the requirements of the gospel, as given in Acts 10:43, *'To Him all the prophets witness that, through His name, whoever believes in Him will receive remission of sins'* and Acts 2:38, *'Then Peter said to them, "Repent, and let every one of you be baptized in the name of Jesus Christ for the remission of sins; and you shall receive the gift of the Holy Spirit."'*

Learning from Observation

After reading of the many fruitful extended revival meetings held in the USA by our evangelists during the late 19th and early 20th centuries, I was convinced that I had to go to America to see and hear first-hand some of these successful preachers. I knew that hundreds of lost souls were being saved during their crusade meetings.

One notable American evangelist and a mentor for my evangelistic ministry, was a man by the name of Dr Jesse Randolph Kellems (who passed to glory in 1980). I had read one of his books and from the words penned by this notable author, I knew I needed to learn how to more effectively preach the gospel and tell of God's forgiveness for sins.

After arriving in the States, it was a great surprise for me to find that this renowned author and dynamic evangelist was still living.

It was an even greater privilege to be invited to share a meal with him and spend time at the church where he was ministering in Los Angeles.

At this time, my wife and our two small children were visiting with my parents on the farm at Bexhill. Joyce's doctor had prescribed the need for her to take a break to help her recover from what he thought was a nervous, upset stomach. The diagnosis later turned out to be wrong, for we soon discovered another baby was on its way!

However, without knowing that Joyce was pregnant, I started to make enquiries and plans on how I could get to America. It could be said that this was the easy part! The hard part was how to find a way to put my plan into place, when I had no money to cover the cost of such a venture.

A contact had told me that the *Kristin Bakke* (a freighter owned by the Knudsen Line out of Norway), was docked in Perth and taking on deckhands. I knew that if accepted, it would be possible for me to work my passage to America. However, I was also told that the Knudsen Line was the last company to be making such travel possible.

Moving Mountains and Uprooting Fig Trees

The *Kristin Bakke* was scheduled to leave Fremantle to sail south of the state to Albany. There they would take on board some 3,000 live sheep destined for the Malaysian markets. The ship was then due to dock back in Fremantle, before sailing to Malaysia, Hong Kong, several ports in Japan and finally to America.

I saw this as my big chance!

My first thought was for Joyce and the children, but my parents agreed to take care of them. Then the Narembeen church where I was ministering at the time agreed to release me to undertake the journey. However, much bigger challenges still confronted me:

obtaining a passport; getting my inoculations; being successful in my application to work on the ship—and all this before the ship was due to sail to Hong Kong in the space of a little more than one week.

As I write these events they sound impossible, but with God preparing the way for me, He really did move mountains!

To be able to apply for a passport, first it was necessary for my father in Lismore to locate my birth certificate and forward it to me in Western Australia by 'snail mail'. Praise God, I received the birth certificate in record time! I then had to forward my application for a passport and visa to Canberra, once more by 'snail mail'. Amazingly, the government-approved documents were returned to me within an unbelievably short turnaround!

My inoculations were proceeding well, but I was told by my doctor that if the first injection didn't work, a follow-up shot would be required after two weeks.

Three Knocks on the Door

As I sourced ways to achieve my goal, one seaman with whom I spoke told me that getting a job on the *Kristen Bakke* was going to be difficult, because the full quota of deckhands had already been signed on before the ship left for Albany. I went to the Seaman's Union, but they were unable to help me! Things were now looking rather grim! However, I believed that this journey was God's call on my life and when the *Kristin Bakke* returned to Fremantle, I boarded the ship and asked the First Mate if he could sign me on as a deck-hand. 'No, I have signed on all the men I need', was his reply.

To be put off so easily went against my nature, so I decided to go and speak to the Chief Engineer to ask if he would sign me on as a 'grease-monkey'. Again, I received a refusal! While we were talking, the Captain of the ship walked out onto the deck and the Chief Engineer said, 'There's the Old Man—ask him'.

So I did, simply and honestly telling him the reason why I wanted to go to America. He called down to the First Mate and said, 'Sign him on as an extra deckhand to look after the sheep'.

Ever since that day, I have always believed that before giving up, we should knock three times for God to open, or close, the door.

However, there was still one more hurdle to jump—my last inoculation! Thankfully, my doctor agreed for me to board the ship, provided the ship's medical officer saw me in the designated two weeks' timeframe. I am not sure what the ship's doctor could have done if my first shot had not taken and I had contracted any of the possible diseases. Perhaps what they did to Jonah! Throw me overboard!

Unmistakably, for all of these requirements for travel to fall into place in such a short space of time, was nothing short of God's hand in action.

But this is just background information for what I am about to share.

God's Connections

I left Australia with only one forwarding address for my mail, so my connections were very limited. When the ship finally docked in Japan, I was so thankful to be able to meet up with the faithful American missionary, Isabel Maxey Dittemore, who served God for over 40 years in Asia. During our time of sharing, Isabel put me in contact with another American missionary, Martin Clark, who was working in Tokyo.

Martin and I spent many hours sharing our beliefs and backgrounds. Finally, he was obviously convinced that I was genuine, 'true blue', or as we Aussies say, 'fair dinkum', and he gave me the phone number of a preacher in Puget Sound, Washington.

On arrival in Vancouver, Canada, and before leaving the ship, I called the contact Martin had given me. Ernest Chamberlain answered the phone, but he explained that where he lived was too far away for him to come and collect me. However, he gave me the phone number of Don Albert, a missionary who was working in Vancouver.

When I called Don he said, 'Wait there and I will come and pick you up'. As I disembarked the ship, two men were on the dock waiting to collect me. The second man was Jim Phillips, the preacher of the Church of Christ in Turlock, central California.

Jim and his wife had adopted a Canadian child and had originally planned to cross over into the United States some 2,000 miles east of where we were in Vancouver. However, when they went to collect the boy's papers, they were told by immigration staff that his papers had been sent to Vancouver. Travelling across Canada to Vancouver, they stayed with Don Albert the very night before I arrived from Perth. I had been at sea for six weeks!

The following day, Jim and his wife drove me across the border, and dropped me off at the Cottage Grove Men's Camp in Eugene, Oregon.

It was here that I met several preachers and evangelists—men whose sermons I had read, but never dreamed that I would ever meet face-to-face. Before Jim left the camp that day, he invited me to come and preach at the church in Turlock.

As a result of the connections made at the camp, a long and fruitful life and ministry was born and several lifetime friendships began, including my friendship with Boyce Mouton, a faithful preacher of the gospel. To this day, we still share in prayer and often exchange insights into God's word.

My return flight to Australia had been paid for out of the generous freewill offerings which were given by churches across the States where I was invited to share and preach during my five months' stay in America.

A year later, in 1961, I once again travelled to America to conduct a crusade for the Turlock church. The Vernon Brothers graciously loaned me the funds for my airfare so that I could return to the States. In the early days of television, these four brothers, together with their wives and children presented a popular TV series through Universal Studies called *Homestead USA*. The program which ran every Sunday evening gained recognition due to their gifted singing, the life situations shared and the talented Bible dramatization. These wonderful godly people became close, lifelong friends.

(In the mid 1990's I invited the Vernon Brothers to travel to Australia to conduct an evangelistic tour. The scheduled itinerary saw the four men and their wives travel throughout northern New South Wales and Queensland, preaching and sharing the gospel in song).

While I was in Turlock, a newly found brother in Christ, Dr Wayne Bigelow, handed me a photo from the local paper of an air-inflated tent. He asked me if such a tent would be helpful for my ministry in Australia. When I replied in the affirmative, the church at Turlock raised the funds and purchased the tent and shipped it to Western Australia. On its arrival, some members from the church at Narembeen provided the funds to pay for the internal fittings.

In 1962, as a result of my wonderful God-given connections in the States, the air-inflated tent was erected for the first time in the suburb of Scarborough. Following this initial *trial* of the tent, now known as 'The Aerosphere', the first crusade was held in Kellerberrin.

Following this, I was blessed to be able to conduct many more crusades in every state of Australia. For two decades I presented the way of salvation to countless numbers of people, thus fulfilling my God-given calling.

Without the divinely planned connections with these godly men and women in Japan, Vancouver and America, I truly believe that my future evangelistic ministries would not have come to fruition.

Over the following years, on so many occasions, on the very morning that I was leaving to go overseas to preach the gospel, it was awe-inspiring for me to find that my set Bible reading for that day would include Psalm 121:8, *'The LORD shall preserve your going out and your coming in from this time forth, and even forevermore.'*

May the Lord be magnified! What a comfort and assurance this verse was for me as I set forth once more to the *fields white unto harvest.*

> *'For all the promises of God in Him are Yes, and in Him Amen, to the glory of God through us.'*
>
> **2 Corinthians 1:20**

1960—Doug disembarking from the Kristin Bakke in Vancouver, Canada

The Vernons—Homestead USA (through Universal Studios)

ONE IN A BILLION

'The preparations of the heart belong to man, but the answer of the tongue is from the LORD.'

Proverbs 16:1

ONCE, WHEN PASSING THROUGH New Delhi, India, I found reasonably priced accommodation at the YWCA and stayed there overnight. For no apparent reason, the next morning when I was checking out, the receptionist read my name out aloud, so that everyone in the reception office heard.

But before sharing with you the amazing thing that then took place, first a little background to this event!

On several occasions I have enjoyed the privilege of working with the American singing evangelists, Janice and Faye Rostvit. *The Rostvit Twins* have memorized songs in over 100 different languages, so that they can share the good news of Jesus in the native tongue of the people they are reaching out to with the gospel.

Janice and Faye had often talked to me about a fellow American missionary, Bernie Getter, with whom they had worked during their many visits to India. They also shared with me that they had told Bernie about me! So, both Bernie and I had developed a mutual respect for each other's ministries, even though we had never met.

The Getters have spent practically their entire working life among the poor people of central India. Their godly labour among these downtrodden people is something many Indian politicians do not like. As a result, the government has made several attempts to cancel their missionary visa, but thankfully each legal challenge in the past has failed.

Nevertheless, the very week of my visit to north India, the Getters were in court once again and this time they were told that their visa renewal application would not be approved.

Now, remember Bernie and I had never met or seen each other, so when the cashier settling my account read out my name, there was an immediate reaction! Standing beside me at the desk was a tall, bearded, Indian-looking man, who turned to me and asked, 'Are you really the Australian evangelist, Doug Willis'?

When I responded in the affirmative, he introduced himself as the American missionary, Bernie Getter. He then took me over to where his wife was sitting and introduced me, saying how sad they were at having had their visa application denied. As we shared together, I was able to pray with them and minister to them in their hour of need for Christian fellowship.

My thoughts have often reflected on how easily I could have stood right beside my fellow brother in Christ that day, and gone on my way without even knowing he was there, or knowing his need. Such reflection leaves me marvelling at God's providence! Why did the cashier speak my name aloud that day when there was no need for him to do so?

And, by the way, amazingly the Getters continue, through God's providence, protection and provision, to serve their Lord in India.

'The lot is cast into the lap, but its every decision is from the LORD.'

Proverbs 16:33

The Rostvit Twins in their early days of ministry

2008—Janice & Faye in Australia—Doug's co-workers both nationally and internationally

CRIME SCENE IN VENEZUELA

'But you be watchful in all things, endure afflictions, do the work of an evangelist, fulfil your ministry.'

2 Timothy 4:5

IT ALL BEGAN WHEN Reggie Thomas received a request from a preacher of a small church in Venezuela, South America, asking him to send someone to teach him the doctrines of the New Testament church. Reggie contacted me and asked me if I would be prepared to take on this mission. I responded positively!

After arriving in the capital, Caracas, I found a bus travelling up-country to the city where our contact lived and ministered. There was one problem, I had no idea where or how to find him.

After making several enquiries at various churches, it seemed that no one knew my contact!

Finally, someone suggested that I enquire at the Police Station. On arrival, I discovered that one of the policemen spoke English. My limited information allowed me to provide him with a rather vague description: a name and what my contact did! To my amazement, the officer replied that he thought he knew the man! I was very thankful for his response; for it appeared some progress was being made in my search.

Yet another surprise! The officer then offered to drive me to my contact's home, which he said was on the other side of the city. I happily sat in the back of the two-door police car, quietly thanking God that the officers were assisting me to get to my destination. We had not gone far, when a call came over the two-way radio, directing the police to attend a robbery that was in progress at a jewellery store in the CBD.

I held my breath and prayed as we made a 'fast and furious' drive to the location, finally coming to a screaming halt. The two policemen hopped out of the vehicle and ran into the store, leaving me stuck in the back seat of the car with no quick means of escape.

When the officers returned to the vehicle I was told that the thieves had escaped and after the short time needed for them to finish their paperwork, we continued on our way to where the officer thought my contact lived.

It was quite a relief to find that the policeman had indeed taken me to the very person I had been asked to meet and teach. After some explanation of why I had arrived in a police car and that I had come as a result of his request to Reggie Thomas, I shared a blessed and fruitful time with his family and the small church.

How great is our God! He is wonderful and He is so very compassionate to His servants.

'You shall not be afraid of the terror by night, nor of the arrow that flies by day, nor of the pestilence that walks in darkness, nor of the destruction that lays waste at noonday. A thousand may fall at your side, and ten thousand at your right hand; but it shall not come near you.'

Psalm 91:5-7

Reggie Thomas, Founder and Director of WFOE (Joplin, MO)

BALLARAT'S 'PRAYER LOG' CRUSADE

'Again I say to you that if two of you agree on earth concerning anything that they ask, it will be done for them by My Father in heaven. For where two or three are gathered together in My name, I am there in the midst of them.'

Matthew 18:19-20

IN 1962, PEEL STREET Church of Christ in Ballarat, Victoria, invited me to conduct an aerosphere crusade in their city. The organizers chose a site for the aerosphere and gave the crusade the title of *Space-age Crusade*. The four other Churches of Christ in the Ballarat district joined hands in hosting, organising and supporting the five-week crusade.

There were many blessings as a result of the gospel meetings conducted during that crusade. On the second Sunday night, my sermon was titled, *What Must I Do to Be Saved?* We had barely started to sing the invitation song at the close of my message, when 12 people came forward from various parts of the crowded tent to surrender their lives to Christ and make a public confession of their faith.

The aerosphere typically seated 400 people, but on this Sunday night some 500 people had crammed inside. Due to the large crowds that were beginning to attend the meetings and the obvious need to provide additional seating, the organizers had discussed with me the various safety issues involved with the aerosphere. It was decided that for the remaining Sunday night meetings, we would hire one of the local theatres, because of its ability to seat 750 people.

On the last Sunday night meeting of the crusade, the balcony was opened so that we could accommodate the big crowd and that night 30 more people came forward in response to the gospel invitation.

During the crusade we had organized early-morning prayer meetings in several homes across the city. Each day, before going about their normal activities, many faithful brothers and sisters met together in one of these locations to pray for the salvation of lost souls.

On the last Friday night, as the crusade was drawing to a close, we arranged for those who had been attending the daily prayer meetings to come together after the meeting in one of their homes.

Prayer Log Felled!

That morning I had gone with the son of the Peel Street preacher and cut down a tree on a hillside on the edge of the city. When everyone had arrived at the house that night, we announced that we were going to go out to the site to conduct a weekend of prayer and intercession for the lost. We invited all who could to join us!

It was our intention to have at least two people at the prayer log at all times, right up until the close of the Sunday night meeting. Because we never held Saturday night gospel meetings, those who were committed to being involved would be free to pray the rest of Friday night—then continue in prayer right through to the close of the Crusade. The only exception to this plan would be on Sunday morning, so that everyone would be free to attend the Breaking of Bread meeting.

At the log we had placed a sheet of butcher's paper on a board, with two columns and two headings. The first column allowed people to write the name of a relative or friend who they knew needed to be saved. The second column was a place where they could write the name of someone they knew who had fallen away from Christ and His church—and needed to be restored! The board was then placed in a position where all those kneeling at the log could read each of the names that had been provided.

Over the weekend, as the church members heard about the 'prayer log' on 'prayer hill', others also made their way up to join us in prayer and to write the name of a friend or loved one on the board!

By late Saturday night the prayer warriors had completely filled the board with many names, and, as planned, at least two people (and sometimes many more), were at the prayer log at all times—ensuring there was no break in the prayer chain.

Whilst I was praying at the log late Saturday night and early Sunday morning, an overwhelming sense of assurance came over me! The Holy Spirit had laid on my heart the words of Jesus in Mark 11:24, *'Therefore I say to you, whatever things you ask when you pray, believe that you receive them, and you will have them.'*

I was no longer *asking* God! Instead, I started *thanking* God for the amazing things I knew He was going to do in the meetings that Sunday.

The Final Sunday

On Sunday morning the five local churches all joined together for the Breaking of Bread meeting. Over 600 people gathered and the aerosphere overflowed.

The Dawson Street preacher had specifically asked me to finish the meeting by midday! But, as the morning proceeded the singing was magnificent; the communion meditation was given by a local preacher; and a thanksgiving offering was taken. Then followed the Bible readings and a choral item by the York Street Choir (joined by members from the other host churches). By the time I stood to preach, it was already noon!

At the end of my message I gave the invitation for any unsaved person present to come forward and confess their faith in Christ. I also asked for any who had backslidden to repent and re-dedicate their lives to the Lord.

It has rarely been my practice to keep a detailed account of the number of conversions at my crusades, but I am just a little sorry now that no one counted the number of those who came forward that Sunday morning. I know that 30 people could stand side by side across the breadth of the aerosphere and there were three rows before me, plus people standing in the aisles.

Cecil Jackel, the Peel Street preacher at that time, came forward to the microphone and publicly made his own re-commitment to Christ. He concluded his testimony by stating, 'This is the nearest thing I have ever seen to a revival'.

Later many testimonies of changed lives were shared as a result of this crusade, especially from this last Sunday morning. There is a saying, 'Satan trembles when he sees the weakest saint upon his knees'.

At the close of the Sunday night meeting, together with a number of the faithful prayer warriors, I went back to join those who had remained on prayer hill, so that we could continue giving thanks and praise to our prayer-answering God.

What a joy and privilege it will be to be numbered among the following: *Those who are wise shall shine like the brightness of the firmament, and those who turn many to righteousness like the stars forever and ever'* (Daniel 12:3).

> *'Now this is the confidence that we have in Him, that if we ask anything according to His will, He hears us. And if we know that He hears us, whatever we ask, we know that we have the petitions that we have asked of Him.'*
>
> **1 John 5:14-15**

1962—the first aerosphere crusade was held in Kellerberrin, Western Australia

1962—inside the aerosphere, fitted-out by members of the Church of Christ at Narembeen

TO RUSSIA WITH LOVE

'No evil shall befall you, nor shall any plague come near your dwelling.'

Psalm 91:10

REVIVAL FIRES MINISTRY OUT of Joplin, Missouri, organised my first trip to Russia in 1991. They decided to call the crusade *To Russia with Love*.

The remains of everyday life under communism were still notably evident almost everywhere that I went on this first visit. The communist government had demolished practically all of the privately-owned houses after coming to power in 1917. Families still lived in government apartments, and regardless of any weather changes, the heaters were turned on by a central control on the day assigned to a specific area.

People still queued up in government stores to buy limited food items. A government landline and speaker had been placed in every apartment, but there were no controls! Of course, the content of any broadcast was only what the government wanted the people to hear!

As a result of the Chernobyl radiation fall-out, the streets in the southern cities were still being washed down each morning. My volunteer assignment took me to Bryansk, one of these southern cities, 379 kilometres south of Moscow.

A university student, Andrew Murygin, had been assigned to me as a translator! He was the son of an officer in the Red Army and had made his decision for Christ under the ministry of a Campus for Christ Crusade.

My meetings in Bryansk were held in the Town Hall. During the week of the crusade, several came forward at the close of the gospel message to confess their faith in Christ.

On Saturday morning I hired a small bus to take those who were to be baptized, together with my translator and other crusade workers, to find a suitable place to conduct the baptisms. As we started our journey I asked where we were heading: The reply was that we were travelling out into the forest! I was told that baptisms were normally held away from prying eyes (atheistic communism opposed all aspects of public, political and religious beliefs in the everyday life of its citizens)!

As we started on our journey, I looked out the window of the bus and saw a lake close to the centre of town: The banks of the lake were crowded with bathers. I asked Andrew why we could not hold the baptisms there! At my query, those in the bus looked at me somewhat astonished! Actually, I now know they were really all a little stunned at what I had suggested, but no one objected. So, we turned the vehicle around and headed back to the lake!

As we led the first candidate down to the water, we asked the bathers seated on the bank if we could have a few moments of quiet reverence while we conducted the baptisms. I recall that there were 16 converts who were to be baptized that day!

After baptizing these precious souls, my translator amazed me by requesting that I baptize him. Unbeknown to me, whilst I knew that he had given his life to Christ, I did not know that he had never been taught, until then, to obey the Biblical command to be immersed.

(It is a joy to my soul to know that today Andrew is a leading member of a Church of Christ in Moscow and a successful lawyer and partner in a prominent law firm).

As I stood in the crisp waters of the lake that day I began preaching to the many people who came around the lake's edge to witness the baptisms.

Then it happened!

People started coming down in their bathers requesting to be baptized. My question to each one as they came forward was, 'Are you willing to repent and trust Christ for your salvation'? When these people replied with the confession, 'I believe that Jesus Christ is the Son of God', we proceeded to baptize them.

And they kept coming!

Finally one of our team asked the question, 'Are we doing the right thing'? To our knowledge, none of those who were coming forward had attended any of the crusade meetings.

As I continued preaching and appealing to those listening between the ongoing baptisms, our translator asked the next person who came forward, 'Why are the people coming for baptism'?

The answer was as thrilling as it was astounding, for we were told, 'For some time now we have been secretly listening to short-wave Christian radio broadcasts out of Canada. We have just been waiting for someone to come and baptize us'.

What a wonderful privilege was mine that day! I am so thankful that the fear of being affected by radiation did not prevent me from taking up the challenge to preach in Bryansk.

Another unexpected, beautiful thing happened while we were conducting the baptisms! A young deaf and dumb man came down from the bank indicating that he wanted us to baptize him. The question in our mind was how could we know if he was genuine in his desire to follow Christ and how could we hear his confession of faith? Andrew, my quick thinking translator came up with the idea of writing the question on the man's hand with his finger. With a big smile on his face, the young man's written reply was a positive, 'Yes'! So the Lord added yet another soul to His church that day.

We did not take a count of the numbers baptized, but I know that I was in the water preaching and baptizing for about an hour.

I do regret that I have no record of the names of those baptized. I have never consciously been aware of seeing any of them again. We pray for them regularly and hope one day to meet some, if not all, in glory.

A Hunger Not Seen in Australia!

On my second visit to Russia (Bryansk) in 1993, I was accompanied by my wife Joyce, together with Brian and June Sprigg. I had baptized Brian in Narembeen during my first ministry after completing my Bible College course.

On this visit, we distributed 2,000 Bibles, plus some beautifully illustrated Bible story books for the children. As we closed one evening meeting, we invited people to come forward to receive a copy of the Bible. Joyce was standing on the floor in front of a high platform handing out the Bibles; however, we had to rescue her from being crushed by the crowd as they surged forward. These dear people were so hungry for a copy of God's word! This 'hunger' is something Australia has never seen! Several told us that they wanted extra copies of the Bible to hide under the floor of their houses, in case atheistic communism returned to Russia.

Some of the converts on this second tour came from the nearby town of Dyatkovo (Crystal City). Vladimir Tyurin was my translator for the second week of this crusade. From its earliest days, Vladimir has been ministering to what is now a strong New Testament congregation. In 2017 he wrote to us advising that the church was about to plant another congregation in Crystal City— the city so famous for its vast production of beautiful, quality crystal.

In John 4:1[b] we read that *'Jesus made and baptized more disciples than John.'* Should we not strive to do the same?

'Then Crispus, the ruler of the synagogue, believed on the
Lord with all his household. And many of the Corinthians,
hearing, believed and were baptized.'

Acts 18:8

1991—Onlookers gather around to watch the baptisms

1991—Doug with some of the newly baptized converts

1993—Doug with some new converts—Andrew is crouched in the front left

2019—Vladimir with his wife and children

GOD'S 'ONE HUNDREDFOLD'!

'Then Peter began to say to Him, "See, we have left all and followed You." So Jesus answered and said, "Assuredly, I say to you, there is no one who has left house or brothers or sisters or father or mother or wife or children or lands, for My sake and the gospel's, who shall not receive a hundredfold now in this time—houses and brothers and sisters and mothers and children and lands, with persecutions—and in the age to come, eternal life."'

Mark 10:28-30

God's Provision of Housing

HAVING MARRIED IN 1957 at the beginning of my final year in Bible College, I still had no idea where Joyce and I would live!

Thankfully, while still on our honeymoon the Principal of the College, AW Stevenson, contacted my home-town preacher, Arnold C Caldicott, and advised him that arrangements had been made for me to minister at the church in Wiley Park, Sydney and occupy the flat attached to the back of the chapel. We gratefully accepted this invitation and praised God for this timely lesson in trust.

Our next home was in Narembeen in Western Australia. The Manse was located right behind the church building and on our arrival we settled into the next chapter of our lives—a full-time church ministry!

It was not long before we understood that ministry is not just about a sermon or two on Sundays, but ministry is being available to the congregation 24/7—a valuable lesson for us to take on board for the future.

Over the years to follow, while conducting crusades, housing was often unexpectedly provided. I recall that while in Victoria conducting a five-week aerosphere crusade at Thomson, Geelong, the church at Latrobe Terrace not only sponsored the crusade, but also provided a house for us to live in for the period of the meetings and for a short time afterwards.

Victorian weather is renowned for being changeable and at this time our first child, Mark, had just started school. One afternoon the fog was still so thick at three in the afternoon that Joyce had to walk to school and meet him, so she could guide him back to our home.

Besides our four children, a lady who needed a lot of care and Christian love was staying with us, together with another young woman, Eve, who was from Ballarat. Eve had volunteered to come and help Joyce with the housework and with minding the children. She was a happy soul, adored by our daughter Deanne and a big help to Joyce during this time of additional need.

We were now standing much stronger in our learned lesson of trust!

One such home was provided by the church in Warwick, Queensland. Their manse was available and in return for its use, between my crusades, I ministered to the church.

When we concluded our ministry in Warwick, the share-farmer's cottage on my father's farm in Bexhill became vacant and my father offered it to us. He was always an encouragement and a supporter of my ministry and he considered this as being part of his contribution to God's work.

We spent four happy years there with the children attending the local school, which was just a couple of country-paddocks away!

Providentially, during the many crusades that followed throughout the eastern states of Australia, without exception, houses 'just happened' to become available for our use.

Even more amazing, this was also the case internationally! When ministering in Dubai, UAE and San Juan Capistrano, California, house-sitting was offered to us just when we needed a place to live.

What's in a Name?

Philip, our fifth child, was born during our time at Bexhill. Close to the time of his birth, I was fulfilling a commitment to conduct a crusade at Inverell, a large country town on the north western slopes of the state.

One morning, I was on my knees in prayer in the kitchen of the house where I was staying, asking the Lord for guidance in naming our yet unborn child. We had no knowledge of the gender of the baby, so it was a surprise to me that the name Philip (as in Philip the evangelist), was indelibly impressed on my mind that morning. I stood to my feet and rang Joyce and told her that we were going to have a boy and that his name would be Philip. She agreed with my decision and we were very thankful to welcome the birth of our fourth son a few weeks later.

The Call of the Outback!

Whilst living at Bexhill, I was invited by the Churches of Christ Queensland Home Missions Committee to become the Northern Missioner for the state.

We were grateful that we were able to put in place with the church at Charters Towers a similar housing arrangement as we had held with the church at Warwick. We would have free use of the manse while I ministered to all of the isolated members scattered throughout the north and north-west of the state. This meant that I could fulfil my commitment as Northern Missioner; evangelize internationally; and when home minister to the local church.

The vast area of outback northern Queensland meant that I had a very large parish indeed! It was a region of the nation where there were no Churches of Christ in place. For me, this calling involved counselling; evangelizing and sharing communion; as well as setting churches in order. It was during this time that the church in Mt Isa was recommenced and new families were added to the congregation.

During home visitations, Christian literature and Bibles were made available to all isolated members, who were always very appreciative of this ministry.

At this time an aerosphere crusade was conducted in Mt Isa with John Timms and an American preacher, John Caldwell, taking the bulk of the meetings. During the crusade, two homeless men came to Christ! One became a faithful member of the church.

A few years ago, I met up with a man whom I had baptized during this period of my ministry: in a farm dam on a property outside of Cloncurry. I rejoiced that he was still faithfully attending church meetings and joining in fellowship around the Lord's Table every week.

Whilst serving as Northern Missioner, Don Paddon, a preacher from my home church in Lismore had penned a story about my outback ministry. It was published in a colourful two-page centrefold of the Queensland *Sunday Mail*. It was titled '*Modern Day John the Baptist*' and included photos of the aerosphere and a convert being baptized in the Moondarra Dam, Mt Isa.

A Philippian Jailer Moment

After a three-year ministry in Charters Towers, I moved my family to Cairns. Initially, a large caravan with an awning was provided by a Christian couple and it became our home for a few months.

On an earlier trip in the outback, I visited Lakeland Downs, a massive maize growing project where the machinery operators on the property worked long 12-hour days. I had been asked to visit one particular woman who was a baptized believer, so that I could share the gospel with her husband, who operated one of the machines. After teaching him the way of salvation, in due course, he decided to receive Christ as his Saviour and Lord. We made our way over to the dam that same night, where he was baptized into Christ.

It was around midnight when we arrived back to their caravan. His wife then prepared a meal of spaghetti bolognaise! Turning to Acts Chapter Sixteen, the conversion of the Philippian jailer and his household, I pointed out the similarities to what had just taken place.

Yes, it was this couple's caravan that was later offered to us when we moved to Cairns and it met a real need for housing at that time!

A Council Condemned House

Houses for rent were very rare in Cairns! After much searching, a condemned house in Scott Street was made available to us. When entering the house for the first time, Joyce had tears in her eyes. Our daughter Deanne comforted her by saying, 'Mum, it will be alright when we get our sunshine and happiness into it'.

While living in Scott Street our son John's involvement and ongoing love for horses began. He was about 11 years old at the time. We woke one morning to find his bed empty, only to discover that he had been up before dawn, and was working down at the stables. He had found himself a job—to save enough money to buy his own horse!

The majority of our son Mark's ministry as a minister of the gospel of Jesus Christ has been as a Chaplain with the Royal Australian Air Force. Whilst his desire and call to ministry was sparked by a visit to our Charters Tower's home by a Missionary Aviation Fellowship aircraft (VH-WET) and pilots, it was his involvement with the Australian Air Force Cadets in Cairns that gave him direction and possibilities. Mark was recognized with an award for the most outstanding Air Cadet in his first year with the organization. Little did he know then, that in 2018 he would become Australia's Principal Air Force Chaplain based in our nation's capital, Canberra.

Crusade Results Come Full Circle!

While ministering in Cairns we saw several souls saved and the church established. We also held an Aerosphere Crusade with

Reggie Thomas as the evangelist: In particular an event that stands out in my mind during this crusade was a young man named Roger Hammond, who made his decision to be baptized into Christ. That night, several of us went to the Barron River and rejoiced with him in his obedience to the Lord.

Roger soon became my travelling companion and assisted me during several of my crusades. He went on to study at a Bible College in America, married and became a faithful preacher of the gospel, ministering in churches both in Australia and New Zealand. He is presently part of the Ministry Team at the Church of Christ in Caloundra, where my son Peter and his wife Vicki are in ministry.

A Home of Our Own

At this time, due to his age, my father decided to sell his farm at Bexhill and gifted us $7,000 to assist in buying a house of our own. Rather than purchasing an established property, we were blessed to have a lady in the church whose husband was a builder. When he knew what we were planning, he offered to build us a high-set house at cost. With the money that had been given to us from my father and funds that Joyce had unexpectedly inherited from her uncle's estate, we were able to purchase a good block of land at 7 Elmire Close—and build the house.

What an exciting time this was! Something we thought would never happen for us had now been provided. This house not only met our needs for the remainder of our time in Cairns, it also allowed us to provide hospitality and accommodation for a number of young people coming up from south-east Queensland for employment. Our guests all became good friends with our family and were also a blessing to the new church.

There was one exception to this! Two 'children of God' cult members, claiming to be Christians, had sought accommodation with us whilst I was on an overseas evangelistic trip. They bunked downstairs until I came home! Not surprisingly, shortly after I had some discussions with them, they moved on!

Following our time of ministry in Cairns, Fred Walters, the man who built the house for us, became a Christian. With his wife, Cecily, they later became overseas missionaries with the Far Eastern Broadcasting Commission (FEBC).

Brisbane's Record Flood

In January 1974 a record flood occurred in Brisbane after three weeks of continual rain. The Brisbane River, which runs through the heart of the city, broke its banks and flooded the surrounding areas. In total there were 16 fatalities; 300 people were injured; 8,000 homes were destroyed; and an estimated AUS$980 million in damages.

Not long before the flood, we had received another ministry calling and had made the move back to Brisbane. House prices were booming at the time and we sold the Cairns house on an elevated market. The funds enabled us to buy a high-set brick house in the Brisbane suburb of Springwood, and praise God we were well above the record flood levels.

At the time we were house-hunting, a group of local Christians were holding mid-week meetings in Springwood—planning to start a new church. They were hoping to purchase a suitable house that would provide accommodation for a preacher and also function as a meeting place for the church.

The day we purchased the house on Springwood Road, I noticed a man sitting in his car on the other side of the road. When he saw me, he came over inquiring about the property and when I told him that we had just bought the house, his countenance visibly fell. He introduced himself as Roger Wall and explained that his church group had been hoping to purchase the property.

When I told him who I was and that we would be happy for the new Church of Christ to meet under our home, he started 'jumping for joy'. Our prayer-answering God had met our need, whilst also meeting the needs of this committed group of Christian brothers and sisters.

Honey I Bought a House

A few other moves, and some years later, we made a decision to live on Bribie Island, some 40 minutes north of Brisbane.

Initially, we rented a house while looking for a place to buy. We had almost given up finding something suitable when an advertisement in the local paper caught my attention. I contacted the agent, who met me at the property and showed me through the house. It was located in the suburb of Bongaree, and the asking price was well within our budget. The house had been neglected over recent years, but had been built by a timber-mill owner, hence it was solid and it had a few very interesting 'nooks and crannies'— one, I decided, would make a good study for me and the other an excellent sewing and craft room for Joyce.

Whilst the agent was showing me the house, I noted that there was another couple sitting outside waiting to inspect the property. Because we had been house-hunting for so long and we had looked at so many properties, I resolved that rather than risk losing the opportunity, I would make an on-the-spot decision to buy!

When I went home, Joyce asked me what I thought of the house! After describing it to her and hedging around the topic somewhat, I finally said, 'Honey, I bought the house'!

Of course her reaction was to say, 'You did what'?

I responded quickly by taking her to inspect the house, hoping and praying that she would like it. As soon as she walked inside she said, 'I love it'!

I sighed in relief, but then—I knew she would!

With the funds left over from the initial purchase price, we were able to do some effective renovations and improvements. The house proved to be a great blessing to us.

On selling the property at Bexhill to make the move to Bribie Island, the person who bought our house told us that when she came to inspect the home she felt a beautiful presence inside. After Joyce died, a similar comment was made by the young couple who bought our Bribie Island home. An added bonus to the character of this home was the two glass sliding doors that had been sand-blasted by Tom Farrell, a Christian brother and gifted artisan. The doors portrayed an eagle and the Scripture passage from Isaiah 40:31, *'They shall mount up with wings like eagles . . .'*

I know that it was only because of God's provision that all these things came to pass, because living as a faith missionary does not provide excess money to put aside for buying real estate. God has always provided for our every need. We are told that if we forsake earthly things, He will take care of His servants and their needs—for us, this was surely God's 'one hundredfold'!

> *'Can a woman forget her nursing child, and not have compassion on the son of her womb? Surely they may forget, yet I will not forget you.'*
>
> **Isaiah 49:15**

MISSION IMPOSSIBLE–ALMOST!

'So Jesus said to them, "Because of your unbelief; for assuredly, I say to you, if you have faith as a mustard seed, you will say to this mountain, 'Move from here to there,' and it will move; and nothing will be impossible for you."'

Matthew 17:20

Up the Birdsville Track

THE TASK OF TAKING five American preachers up the legendary Birdsville Track was an incredible experience of survival—and if the Lord had not been on our side, a mission impossible!

The track in the 1970's was an isolated 517 kilometres of dirt road and sand that traverses three deserts along the route: the Strzelecki, Sturt Stony and Tirari Deserts. Entering the track at Marree, South Australia we were advised to let the local police know of our intentions and report in at Birdsville, Queensland upon our arrival: that is, if we made it through—lives had previously been lost on the track!

The journey from Adelaide to Mt Isa is a total of 3,457 kilometres. The track passes through one of the driest parts of Australia, with an average rainfall of only 100 millimetres a year. The area is extremely barren, dry and isolated, and travellers must always carry water and other supplies in case of emergencies.

At times the sandy track disappeared and we had to make our own road in the direction we were travelling. We were trusting that God was watching over us and it was a wonderful opportunity for these visitors to travel through the 'real' Australian outback.

Among the preachers were Dr Blythe Robinson and Dr John Caldwell. At one spot in the road, the sheer uninhabited and wild environment prompted John to christen the region, 'The abomination of desolation'.

On the journey we shot a kangaroo (roo) for our evening meal and Blythe, who had borrowed my white shoes, managed to get blood all over them. Despite this, Blythe and I became close friends during his visit to Australia and we still are to this day. We have shared several international mission trips together as co-workers, networking with WFOE.

The five men were part of the Revival Fires Team that toured Australia in 1970 following the World Convention of Churches of Christ in Adelaide. One-by-one I dropped them off at planned preaching points all the way from Mt Isa to Cairns, a distance of over 1,250 kilometres (in all, the total trip covered on this mission was 4,707 kilometres).

Call the Mission Team

Another amazing trip through the northern Peninsula of Queensland was organised by a brother attending the Charters Towers church when we were ministering there. Roger had a Willys Jeep and was married to an indigenous lady.

We planned a trip that went up to the north of Cape York Peninsular, with the intention of visiting all the aboriginal communities from Cairns to Thursday Island. We were accompanied on this mission by Lyle Morris, who has spent most of his life ministering to indigenous Australians.

My role was to supply food for the three-week, 3,000 kilometre trip. The plan was to get our supply of fresh meat by killing wild pigs, turkeys, ducks and wallabies on the way. This supply of meat would complement our ration of fruit, nuts and tinned sardines.

We left Cairns and travelled via Laura, then left the sealed road at Coen to travel the Post Master General's (PMG) track directly north to Bamaga.

Bamaga is located at the very top of the Peninsula near Possession Island where Captain Cook claimed Australia for the British Crown. The route took us through many creek crossings and countless gullies so deep that we had to winch our way out of the many bogs.

We were told that no vehicles had travelled over the track for about six months, due to the big wet that year. Hence, some of the trails into the aboriginal mission stations were overgrown with saplings which we had to either knock or cut down to get through.

Due to the big wet, water was still high in some of the creeks. We only had a manual operated winch to haul our vehicle through the boggy gullies and during the journey we joked together that when we returned home we would declare that we were the fittest preachers in Queensland. Some river banks were deeply gutted and precarious to negotiate and with only one vehicle, almost impossible!

As we neared the top of the Peninsula we discovered that the Jardine River was still flooded. To our surprise, we found that one group had arrived at the crossing ahead of us. However, the reason for their success was soon understood, because they were the famous Leyland Brothers of TV fame. They had two vehicles fully equipped with all the latest outback gear one could ever imagine.

We were aware that they were watching as the three of us set out to wade the rather wide river. With the river running fast, we were very relieved to hear one of them call out and offer to take us across in their boat.

Once across the river, we set out on foot to walk the remaining 40 kilometres into Bamaga. Thankfully, we had only gone a little way down the road when we came across some council workers who offered to drive us into town after they finished work. We did not mind the long wait as it was in exchange for a ride!

We took a ferry across to Thursday Island to do some visitation: From there, I hitched a boat ride across to Prince of Wales Island. An American farmer had leased the island and had shipped his beef herd by barge from Townsville. His wife was a baptized believer and her name was on my isolated members' list. On arrival, I had to hop out of the boat and wade through the shallow water for the final leg, as the fluctuating tides did not allow the boats to go all the way into the shore at low tide.

I arrived on the island on a Sunday, so I announced to my hosts that I had come to conduct a communion service. They no doubt were very surprised at my arrival, for I had been unable to contact them to let them know of my intention to visit. However, they were very welcoming and thankful that I was able to call on them to share in fellowship.

Once this visit was over, I managed to get a ride back to Thursday Island and then on to Bamaga to join my two friends.

On the way home, we enjoyed a stop-over at the aluminium mining town of Weipa where we bought and ate a whole two-litre carton of ice cream. This treat was a real luxury after the rations we had been living on for the past weeks.

It was a wonderful blessing for us to be able to visit all of the indigenous mission stations on the Peninsula, except one. For them the blessings came as we taught the children at their school assemblies and distributed a lot of Christian magazines and indigenous-designed tracts.

'No grave trouble will overtake the righteous, but the wicked shall be filled with evil.'

Proverbs 12:21

WHO TURNED THE CAR AROUND?

'But our God is in heaven; He does whatever He pleases.'
Psalm 115:3

WHILE GOD'S DWELLING PLACE is in Heaven, yet we know He is with us every day through the presence of the Holy Spirit. I recall many occasions when God's leading was powerfully evident and the events had an overwhelming impact on my life: Two in particular stand out!

During my crusades it was always my habit to collect the names and addresses of the people who were attending the meetings. The following day I would pray over these contacts and as I was writing them down I would rank them according to what I considered were the people in most need. I did this so I could visit them in a prioritized order.

During a crusade in Perth I was driving down a road to visit the first person on my list. As I journeyed, I drove past the street where another contact lived. At that moment, I experienced a strong leading to go and visit her first, but I tried to keep driving in the direction I was going, thinking that it was just a spontaneous thought. But the urge was so strong that I had no option! I had to turn around and go back to the street where the woman lived. When I knocked on the door, the lady opened it and exclaimed, 'Oh, Mr Willis, you are just the person I want to talk to. How can I become a Christian'?

Even to this day, so many years later, I recall her house. Such a beautiful home! It had been built by her husband, who was a butcher by trade. I remember a large glass wall that overlooked the Swan River and underneath the internal staircase there was a water feature containing a lovely fountain, ferns and lilies. For me, it was such a striking, inspiring setting in which to open the Scriptures and teach this dear soul the way of salvation. Soon after my visit, this lady confessed her faith in Christ and was baptized. I was told that at a later time her husband also obeyed the gospel.

Lord, Which Way Should I Turn?

On the second occasion, the late Rob Holt and I were conducting an aerosphere crusade in Gladstone, Queensland. It was a blessing for Rob that his family was able to accompany him on this trip.

There was a man who was attending the meetings who held an important position in a denominational church in town. Because of his apparent commitment and involvement with this congregation, I placed his name on the bottom of my list of visitations that day. The non-church-going contacts were always intentionally placed first on my list!

On leaving my accommodation that morning, I drove around the corner to turn right in order to make my first visit. Once again a strong leading came over me to turn left and visit *first* the man whom I had placed *last* on my list. For a time, I sat in the car 'arguing with the Lord': This, of course, is not a good thing to do! I told myself, and the Lord, that there was no point in calling on this man, because he would definitely be at work! Furthermore, he was an active member and an important office-bearer within his congregation.

However, knowing that God is always in control, and after a few more minutes sitting by the side of the road, I found it impossible to turn right. Still arguing to myself, I drove up to the man's house and opened the front gate. Even while walking down the path to the front door I was silently saying to myself, 'This is crazy, the man is at work. He will not be home'.

You can imagine my shock when, after knocking, the man opened the door and said, 'Oh, Doug you are just the person I want to see. Please come in'.

Before long, he opened up his heart to me and confessed that he knew he was not saved.

A Cornelius Moment

What a God-given opportunity!

Here was an active church-going man who knew he was not 'born anew from above'. I opened my Bible and for the next hour I shared with him the gospel and God's requirements for salvation. I recall vividly turning in my Bible to Acts Chapter 10 and reading the account of another man who was very religious: a God-fearing man; a man who was known as a just and devout person; a man who always prayed; a man who fasted; a man who gave to the poor; and a man who had a good reputation! But, even so, he was a man in need of salvation!

We then reflected on how God had sent an angel to instruct Cornelius to send for Peter, who would tell him words by which he and his household could be saved. Before leaving, I shared with him the words of Peter in Acts 10:43, *'Whoever believes in Him will receive remission of sins'*, and verse 48, *'And he commanded them to be baptized in the name of the Lord.'*

The man thanked me and expressed how our time of sharing had been a great help to him and that he was so glad that I had visited him that day. I do not know why he was not at work that morning. He was not physically sick! Perhaps he may not have been at home later that day when my plan had been to visit him. But what I do know is that God knew!

God's hand in directing our lives may not always be as significant and as obvious as these two accounts were for me, but I know He is there, behind the scenes, directing our every step. The question remains: Are we walking in the steps He has set before us and are we following His leading?

'And we know that all things work together for good to those who love God, to those who are the called according to His purpose.'

Romans 8:28

GUARDHOUSE INTERROGATION

'But I want you to know, brethren, that the things which happened to me have actually turned out for the furtherance of the gospel, so that it has become evident to the whole palace guard, and to all the rest, that my chains are in Christ; and most of the brethren in the Lord, having become confident by my chains, are much more bold to speak the word without fear.'

Philippians 1:12-14

ON ONE OF MY several tours to Uganda, David Eubanks, who at that time was the President of Johnson Bible College in Tennessee, had asked me to look up one of his contacts, an official in the government.

Uganda had suffered much during two civil wars: From rebel tribes; from the atrocities committed under Idi Amin Dada; and from the evils committed by the president who followed Idi into power.

There were still several roadblocks to pass on the way from the airport at Entebbe, into the capital, Kampala. I think one of the most frightening things that are embedded in my memory from this occasion was the child soldiers! These young boys, with rifles over their shoulders, stopped us and told us to open our bags so that they could search for guns and other contraband goods.

After coming out of Entebbe International Airport, I was met by my co-worker Jehoshaphat Kakooza and we decided to stop at the Presidential House to seek information concerning the where-abouts of David's contact. However, the soldiers at the gate became suspicious and took us into the guardhouse. It was only at a later time that we discovered that they suspected we might be gun-runners for the rebels.

At the guardhouse we were interrogated for two hours. Finally, after much questioning, a soldier returned stating that he had located the person we were seeking and that our enquiry was legiti-mate. So, praise God, we all relaxed! The captain then said to me, 'So, you are a preacher, are you'?

I replied, 'Yes, would you like me to prove it'?

To my surprise he answered, 'Yes, we would love to hear the gospel'.

So, this became another God-given opportunity, as I proceeded to share the gospel and the teachings of the New Testament church to all who were in the guardhouse that day.

Another Cornelius Moment

On another occasion when Joyce and I were in Uganda, we decided to stop on a street in Kampala to talk to some soldiers who were sitting in the back of a truck. As already expressed, under Idi Amin and the president who followed him, the Ugandan soldiers committed untold evil acts of violence against the people. As we stopped, my mind was 'racing' with the knowledge of the many atrocities I knew had taken place.

My Ugandan contact, Wamala (the man who had originally invited WFOE to come into the country to conduct evangelistic crusades) shared his personal story with me. He told me of the day the police came and took his father, a judge, to the police station. They never saw him again!

Sometime after their father had been arrested, his brothers were told of the spot in the 'killing fields' of Idi Amin, where their father's body had been dumped. The two brothers, accompanied by two friends, went to the killing fields to recover his body. In their attempt to do so, the two brothers and one of the other men were shot and killed!

His sickening story continued, as he disclosed that his mother had always attended prayer meetings, something that was forbidden by the Muslim dictator in their region! One day, soldiers arrived at her home with a specific directive to shoot her! His mother begged them to allow her to pray first! They did, and then shot her while she was still on her knees. Wamala's young sister, who was hiding in the woodshed, later related to him what had happened. We were told that this poor girl, having witnessed such an inhumane, brutal act has never been the same.

Several other friends and contacts in that nation have told me numerous similar stories. If the soldiers needed corrugated iron, they would simply come and remove the sheets of iron from the roof of one's house, and if anyone dared to object, they would most likely shoot them.

Rape, murder and pillaging were common daily crimes.

With all this knowledge in the back of my mind, we struck up a conversation with the soldiers in the truck and after sharing the gospel with them, the one who appeared to be in charge asked this penetrating question, 'Can a soldier be born again and be forgiven of all his sins'?

Sharing the gospel and answering similar questions to those asked by these soldiers is not a difficult thing to do in most non-Christian and some Muslim nations: especially those not affected by materialism.

So, I shared with them the conversation Jesus had with Nicodemus about the need to be born again. I then turned to Acts Chapter Ten in my New Testament and my reply was a very definite, 'Yes'. As they listened attentively, I was able to share with them the conversion of the Roman soldier, Cornelius.

When it was time for us to go, I left them with the challenge to become followers of the Christ who died for soldiers, as well as for all people. Oh, and yes, I did leave my New Testament with the soldier in charge!

God can bring amazing blessings out of tragedy! How many of those soldiers have become disciples of Christ? This side of heaven, I have no way of knowing! What I do know is that to this very day there is a faithful witness to the teachings of Christ and His apostles in Uganda. My co-worker and dear friend, Jehoshaphat Kakooza, his son Stephen and now a brother named Isaac, are just three of many others who are faithfully proclaiming the way of salvation in their home nation.

On the Mission Field with My Grandson

In 2002 on another mission tour, I was accompanied by one of my American grandsons, Joshua Willis, together with his friend, Tim Stoner. The boys had just graduated from College and wanted to experience and share on the mission field before entering Ozark Christian College in Joplin. The two young men were a great encouragement to Stephen, who is now studying with Christ's Evangelical Foundation (CEF) to become a preacher.

The trip was a time of great blessing for us all! Prior to continuing on to Uganda (the next leg on our itinerary), Joshua and Tim shared some amazing experiences in India, witnessing hundreds coming to Christ in our nightly village meetings.

These two, enthusiastic young men also had the experience of following in the footsteps of the Apostle Paul and his evangelistic team, when we visited contacts and conducted Bible studies in Macedonia.

Training to Become Evangelists

In January 2016, Isaac emailed me and advised that he had resigned from the denomination he was serving with and had started a New Testament church. He also decided at that time to encourage the students in all of his six Bible Training Centres to enrol and study the two-degree preacher-training course with CEF.

Another recent report was received from Johnmark Ighoradhe, my friend and co-worker in Nigeria: sharing news of his international ministry in Rwanda and Uganda. He wrote, 'During my recent visit, I was told that there are plans to carry out the New Testament teachings and to plant new churches in east Africa'.

At a 2017 preacher training seminar for CEF students, Johnmark spoke on the topic, *Our Commission is a Ministry of Reconciliation* and communicated to his audience that, 'The only ground for reconciliation is the true pattern of Biblical conversion, as revealed in the New Testament'.

For me, this thrilling news from these central and east African nations testifies to the truth that one sows, one waters, another reaps and it is God who gives the increase. How real are the words of our Lord in John 4:37, *'For in this the saying is true: "One sows and another reaps."'*

'But the mercy of the Lord *is from everlasting to everlasting on those who fear Him, and His righteousness to children's children.'*

Psalm 103:17

2002—Doug's grandson Joshua (right) on mission in India

2002—(L to R) John Samuel, Doug, Joshua, Daniel Raj

NIGHTLIFE IN GUYANA

'The LORD your God in your midst, the Mighty One, will save; He will rejoice over you with gladness, He will quiet you with His love, He will rejoice over you with singing.'

Zephaniah 3:17

DURING THE YEARS 1972 to 1985 my calling took me to several nations, including Zimbabwe, India, the Philippines and South Korea, where I conducted crusades and preached the gospel.

In 1986, the Lord challenged me to totally commit my life to full-time overseas evangelism. With the help of Reggie Thomas' ministry, I was able to begin this new calling by going into Guyana, South America, for three months.

Guyana, on the northern coast of South America and part of the Caribbean nations, was at that time a communist state. When I first went there, the nation was bankrupt! The nation's currency was absolutely worthless on the international market. Many medicines for life-threatening illnesses were unavailable, even in the hospitals.

During those three months that I spent in Guyana, I had to endure many hardships.

On more than one occasion, thieves snatched at my wristwatch and my jogging shoes which were hanging from my backpack. These incidents were stressful, but possibly the least of the hardships that I faced. For instance, the pit-toilets were interesting to say the least, as Georgetown is below sea-level and the toilets are tidal!

One night I was conducting a meeting outside the capital of Georgetown. The hour was getting very late, but the congregation seemed to be especially interested in what I was teaching. So, I kept on preaching, even after I knew that the buses had stopped running: The public transport came to a halt at dusk, because it was considered too dangerous to operate after dark.

When the meeting finally closed, I had to face the reality that I did not have enough money to hire a car to take me back to my accommodation. With no other option available, I set out to hitchhike back to town. At that time, hitchhiking was considered risky in the safest of nations, but even by stretching one's imagination, in Guyana the practice was definitely not considered safe. Announcements were heard on the radio daily of crimes that led to the death of someone being murdered during the night!

As I set out in the pitch black that night, a car stopped and the driver offered me a ride. As was my habit, soon after getting into the vehicle, I started sharing the gospel. I had a twofold purpose for adopting this practice! First, it was for the purpose of seeking to lead lost souls to Christ and secondly, it was my purpose to make anyone intent on doing me harm to hopefully feel guilty. Of course, I have no way of knowing if my second reason for this practice ever worked! But on this particular night, when the driver stopped to let me out of his car he said, 'You need to be more careful who you get a ride with', and then drove off! As I closed my eyes that night my thoughts were, 'What a wonderful God we serve'. *The Lord be magnified!*

These events all occurred during a time when there was a lot of tension between the African and Indian populations. Landowners had been bringing Africans to Guyana to work as slaves in the cane fields. After slavery was abolished, the British then transferred east Indians into the country to work as indentured labourers. Most of the indigenous people lived back in the hills by themselves. The tensions between Africans and Indians added to the dangers that were lurking on street corners of the town by night, but I can say that the Lord delivered me out of them all. I took constant comfort in the words from Proverbs 15:3, '*The eyes of the LORD are in every place, keeping watch on the evil and the good.*'

It was during this final part of my first mission in Guyana that I conducted my very first preacher-training seminar. On reflecting, I did not realize then that there would be many more training seminars to follow!

'*God is our refuge and strength, a very present help in trouble.*'
Psalm 46:1

Doug, praising God for another safe arrival back home to Australia!

GOVERNMENT OFFICIALS OVERRULED

'It is better to trust in the LORD than to put confidence in man.'

Psalm 118:8

FOR ONE TO TRUST in government officials to process visa applications speedily is like trusting in *a bad tooth or a foot out of joint*. Nonetheless, I do know that we can be confident that God will provide in our time of need. This truth is very real to me and can be identified by the many occasions that I needed to get my passport and visa approved and back in time to catch my next scheduled flight. Sometimes my trips had short turn-around times! At other times, I needed to first get into a country with my passport, before I could send it off to another government office to get a visa for the next country on my planned itinerary.

On one occasion I had to ask the embassy in Canberra to send my passport with my visa to the Sydney International Airport, so that I could pick it up on my way through from Brisbane. Praise be to God, on my arrival the documents were there waiting for me. On this occasion, I felt that it was my trust in 'a good tooth and a foot well jointed'. However, I have no doubt that God's hand of providence was working behind the scenes. You see, our God is a prayer-answering God, if we can only exercise faith and wait on His timing.

On yet another journey, it was necessary for me to apply to the embassy in Washington, DC, for a visa to enter a Caribbean nation. However, I first needed my passport for my flight from Brisbane to Los Angeles. I was booked on a flight that would then take me to Miami, FL, where I was to catch my next international flight.

I knew that timing was critical for my travel plans, so I couriered my passport to Washington and requested that once approved, my documents be returned by courier to the Concierge Desk at Miami Airport—ready for me to collect on my arrival.

Reggie Thomas had arranged accommodation for me with a Christian family in Miami. On arrival back at the airport, I had just an hour or two before my flight was scheduled to leave. Confidently, I went to the desk and asked if there was a parcel for me. After searching for my parcel, the attendant came back and said, 'Sorry sir, there is nothing for you'. Perhaps this time my trust had come face-to-face with that *'bad tooth and a foot out of joint'*!

I totally believed that God wanted me to go and minister in this Caribbean nation. So, trusting in the power of a God in whom we can find grace in our time of need, a short time later, I went back to the counter and asked the very same man would he please look once more for a parcel addressed to me. Looking somewhat frustrated, he disappeared to search a second time, and to his great surprise and my thankfulness and joy, he found my parcel just around the corner on another desk!

If we are doing God's work, we can expect that the devil will try to stop us! I also believe that if it is not God's work, it could be God trying to stop us! I have faith in the knowledge that if we are doing God's work, we can be confident of His leading. If the door opens, then walk through it! If God doesn't want you to go, He will close the door.

We read in Acts 16:6-7: *'Now when they had gone through Phrygia and the region of Galatia, they were forbidden by the Holy Spirit to preach the word in Asia. After they had come to Mysia, they tried to go into Bithynia, but the Spirit did not permit them.'*

We know that Paul experienced both Satan and God closing doors. In 1 Thessalonians 2:18 we read, *'Therefore we wanted to come to you—even I, Paul, time and again—but Satan hindered us.'*

On a more recent occasion, I sent my passport to Canberra with my application for a visa. The documents needed to be back in Brisbane for me to catch my flight the following Monday. Friday arrived and I still had not received my passport with visa, so I rang and checked with the courier who was to pick up my documents, only to be advised by him that he had not yet been able to collect them. He also told me that the embassy would be closed the next day.

Nevertheless, on hearing my plight, he said he would make a special call to the embassy to check if a staff member was available! Well, someone 'just happened' to be there that Saturday morning and they acted on the courier's request and checked the outgoing mail—and there was my passport with visa! He diplomatically handed it to the courier and on Monday morning I was on my flight.

Such times of testing happened on many occasions during my 60 years in evangelistic ministry. When God calls, God provides in our time of need, especially when we are doing His work.

'My brethren, count it all joy when you fall into various trials,
knowing that the testing of your faith produces patience.'
James 1:2-3

PICKPOCKETS IN THE PHILIPPINES

'In God have I have put my trust: I will not be afraid. What can man do to me?'

Psalm 56:11

SITTING SIDE-BY-SIDE, SQUASHED ON crammed benches in a Filipino jeepney, presents an ideal opportunity for thieves to pick one's pocket. I was the victim of this experience several times, not only in the Philippines, but also in crowded Nigerian and Chad markets and taxis.

On a trip to N'Djamena, the capital of Chad, I was holding a large amount of money that a missionary co-worker had given me to hold while she went into a drapery store. She set out to do some bargaining with the store owner over material that she wanted to purchase to make a suit for her husband! Some thieves must have noticed her handing me the cash and in the following five minutes I was attacked three times. The last attempt was from a man who looked like he held a *Jambiya* (an Arabian dagger) under his sleeve. As I pulled the thief's hand out of my pocket, I thanked the Lord for His protection, and decided it was time for me to leave the markets.

Once, when on mission in Cebu, Philippines, I caught a jeepney to go to Naga on the outskirts of the city. I was staying there with my friends, the Labrado family, who were national workers in the local church. Past pickpocket experiences had taught me not to carry my money in a wallet in my hip pocket, so I had purchased a 'man bag' and placed all my valuables in it, including my passport, airline tickets and money.

For some reason that is now hard for me to understand, when I hopped into the jeepney, I decided it would be safer to put my bag under the seat. Yes, you guessed it! I got out of the jeepney and watched it drive off, before realising that my bag was still under the bench seat!

The next day, without any success, I waited by the side of the road hoping to recognise the jeepney. I then went into the city to see what was involved in getting my passport and airline ticket replaced. I soon discovered that this action would take more time and money than I had available! So, I went and waited at the place where I had caught the jeepney the afternoon before.

Now, if you know the Filipino transport system, you will know how hard it is to pick one specific jeepney from the several hundred that are plying the city streets.

Amazingly, a man, on hearing of my plight, was able to name the jeepney driver that I had used the day before. To my joy, he told me that the man actually lived very near to the Labrado's home. Once back at the house, I called the driver on the phone to ask if he had seen my bag. Of course, we were thinking that by this time, it would have been picked up by some desperate person and be long gone. To my great surprise the driver said, 'Yes, a passenger handed me your bag'.

Imagine the joy when we went to collect the bag and we discovered another wonderful provision of the Lord: All my documents and money were still there! We bowed our heads and thanked God that day for good, honest people!

Other similar pickpocket experiences convinced me that it was time to buy a concealed money belt: I did, and was never robbed again!

'The wicked is ensnared by the transgression of his lips, but the righteous will come through trouble.'
Proverbs 12:13

1986—sharing the gospel on radio in the Philippines

1986—Teaching at a Youth Camp in the Philippines

THROUGH FIRE AND WATER

'When you pass through the waters, I will be with you; and through the rivers, they shall not overflow you. When you walk through the fire, you shall not be burned, nor shall the flame scorch you.'

Isaiah 43:2

ONCE, WHEN TRAVELLING BY taxi in Monrovia, Liberia, to go into the interior to preach the gospel, a fierce storm broke out and the rain 'bucketed' down. The roads into the Liberian interior villages are not good at the best of times, but once flooded they become a treacherous quagmire.

Our taxi almost made it as far as the river, which by now had become a raging torrent. As we slowed down, the water came up over the floor of the vehicle. The driver said, 'Sorry, but I can't go any further', and dumped us all by the side of the flooded road.

I quickly changed from my shoes to *flip-flops* (thongs) and set out after the local men, who were already ahead of me walking on an unseen raised edge of the bridge which spanned some 40-50 metres across. As I followed them across this unseen ledge, the water was rushing past, reaching half-way up my legs. One brother carried my suitcase on his head and praise God, we all made it safely across to the other side.

We then set out to walk the rest of the way to the village where we planned to hold the gospel meetings. Little did I imagine the wonderful outcome of this and other hardships that followed that day!

As we walked, I was very thankful for my thongs, because the road was covered with pebbles. As we passed by one house, a man who was standing out the front noticed my plight and offered me his long *fimbo* (African walking stick). I gladly accepted, with the promise that I would return it to him on my way back.

Continuing on, we came across another small stream with a log-bridge. While crossing over the water, I decided to steady myself with the borrowed fimbo, poking it down to the bottom of the creek for balance. Alas, halfway across, the cane went down into a yawning hole and because I was leaning heavily on it, I quickly, and rather clumsily, followed it into the fast-flowing water.

My first reaction was to save my laptop, which had landed in the water with me. My second concern was for my much-needed thongs, which were floating away under the small log-bridge. My third concern was not to let go of the fimbo, so that I could fulfil my promise to return it to its owner. Thankfully, my thongs caught in some debris and I was able to recover them and upon checking, to my great relief, no water had entered my computer carry-bag, which was completely dry inside! And, yes, I was still holding the fimbo!

By the time we arrived at the village, I was almost dry, but I did not refuse the hot water offered to me by the ladies of the church. The much appreciated 'bucket bath' did warm me up!

The rain continued to pour down and while trying to rest that afternoon on my bed, I quickly discovered that it was impossible to avoid the drips coming through the leaking roof. After striving for some time to unsuccessfully dodge the leaks, I gave in, and just lay on my back and let the water drip onto my chest.

The next day, in the Sunday morning church meeting, a woman testified to what finally convinced her to surrender her life to Christ the night before. She stood and said, 'It was the willingness of this preacher from a faraway land, who came through all the water, walking the long way into our village, eating our local food and putting up with all of our hardships so that he could share the love of Jesus with me and my village.' As she spoke, the word of God from James 1:2 came to mind, *'My brethren, count it all joy when you fall into various trials.'*

Even in our small trials, we can see many blessings, and those blessings enable us to rejoice, even in our times of testing.

A typical bridge in Liberia—the narrow path leading to another village!

INDIA'S DEMONS OVERPOWERED

'You are of God, little children, and have overcome them,
because He who is in you is greater than he who is in the world.'

1 John 4:4

IT WAS LATE IN the evening when we arrived in a forest village in south India. We had come to this village to preach the gospel of redeeming grace! Because we had arrived much later than planned, many of the villagers had already retired for the evening: But this is not a problem in India! Some village men went around and woke those who were asleep and before long they all gathered around to hear the message the team had come to share with them.

Towards the close of my message, a woman, clearly demon-possessed, came rolling forward on the ground, totally under the control of a supernatural power. The local men tried unsuccessfully to hold her down. So frightening was the scene that many of those who had gathered to hear the message scattered in every direction.

About five minutes later, the woman once more began rolling uncontrollably towards me, stopping right at my feet. My translator, the late Robert Devadoss, asked me somewhat nervously, 'Shall we pray now'?

My reply was a definite, 'Yes'.

Up until this time, several of us had been praying silently. Now we publicly asked the Lord to deliver this woman and I then bent down to help lift her up, as her glassy eyes started to return to normal.

The people who had scattered now returned, as they witnessed the power of God in action, for this poor troubled woman was now calm. They came back to hear more of the gospel message. As in every such case of demon-possession that I have experienced, I presented the Gospel to this woman, but she refused to repent and displayed no interest in putting her trust in Christ for salvation.

At the close of the meeting that night some 60 souls confessed their faith in Christ. We sent men to dam-up the canal that fed water to the rice paddies. It took some time to get the pump started and have a sufficient depth of water to baptize (immerse) the converts.

When the team members returned after the baptisms, they requested a Bible for the demon-possessed woman and another for her husband. Their request took me by surprise and I asked why she wanted a Bible. My co-workers told me that while they were waiting for the water to rise sufficiently for the baptisms, one of the team members had explained the gospel more fully to the couple and they had both accepted Christ and obeyed Him in the waters of baptism.

I have travelled much and experienced many things in my years of ministry, but let me tell you these experiences can be very frightening.

I recall the fear that was in my own heart on my first of many experiences of demon-possession. On that occasion, a person totally out of control leapt over a couple of rows of seats to come close to where I was standing at the front of the meeting. The power of Satan is very evident and real when these things occur.

I came to learn long ago never to overlook the power of our prayer-answering God. As His people, our Lord has delivered us from this evil world, just as the Bible says in Colossians 1:13, *'He has delivered us from the power of darkness and conveyed us into the kingdom of the Son of His love.'*

Our mission on one particular evening in India was to evangelize by preaching the gospel in a certain country village. On our arrival we came across some Hindu priests who were trying to exorcise a demon-possessed woman. While we were still seated in the car, the woman came and stood right at my door. As I waited to see what would develop, the question in my mind was: What, or who, had directed her to me?

I understood more fully that day that not only the Lord, but also the devil, knows my name.

One of my co-workers got out of the car and started to pray, asking the Lord to deliver the woman from her demons. Then we presented the gospel not only to this poor woman, but to everyone in that village. How wonderful that God's power is still unlimited and the gospel is still His power unto salvation to everyone who believes.

I believe that it is wrong for us to be obsessed with demons. If one allows an obsession to continue, one could become depressed, or even possessed. The Bible tells us: *'Finally, brethren, whatever things are true, whatever things are noble, whatever things are just, whatever things are pure, whatever things are lovely, whatever things are of good report, if there is any virtue and if there is anything praise-worthy—meditate on these things'* (Philippians 4:8) —a much better practice!

It has been my privilege to visit India on more than 40 different occasions. During this time many close and lasting friendships developed, as we laboured together in the gospel: John Samuel and his son Santhosh; the late MT Timothy and his son Isaac; Ezra Gnanaraj and his father John; Prem Kumar; EK Durairaj; Sridharan John Wesley; Suku Thomas; Paul Ragu; Daniel Raj; Sam Daniel; and many, many others.

I count these godly men among my long-standing friends and co-workers. Together with their gospel teams they encounter many hardships daily, as they take the gospel to the unreached villages of south India.

Working with them has also provided me with the opportunity to conduct numerous preacher-training seminars and conferences and with the support of many faithful sponsors of my ministry, raise the funds to establish and help maintain six Bible Colleges.

One of the many preacher-training seminars conducted in South India

Village Evangelistic Teams

2008—Doug with tribal people in Tamil Nadu, India

*2011—An estimated 1,600 people came in buses,
cars and tractors to attend the Convention*

*Two of the original Indian Village Team
members—Doug's co-workers since 1976
(L to R) The late MT Timothy, Doug and John Samuel*

*Doug presenting Diplomas to Graduates of the Joyce Willis Memorial
Bible College*

*2016—Doug with co-worker and translator Ezra Gnanaraj, Beulah
Christian Church, Chennai,*

UNDENIABLE EVIDENCE

'Since you have purified your souls in obeying the truth through the Spirit in sincere love of the brethren, love one another fervently with a pure heart, having been born again, not of corruptible seed but incorruptible, through the word of God which lives and abides forever.'

1 Peter 1:22-23

I BELIEVE THE GREATEST evidence that a personal God exists is the power of the gospel of Christ to completely transform lives. No doubt this is why the apostle Paul was not ashamed of the gospel, and why we should never be ashamed!

During a crusade held in Byron Bay, New South Wales in the late 1960s, a recently converted man told me that during his life he had broken all the Old Testament commandments—plus more! He continued to share with me that in his conversion, the Lord had saved him, had cleansed his soul, and made him whole.

John W Peterson captured these thoughts so fittingly in his song, *It Took a Miracle*:

My Father is omnipotent, and that you can't deny;
A God of might and miracles, 'tis written in the sky!
The Bible tells us of His power and wisdom all way through;
And every little bird and flower are testimonies too.
The greatness of the Lord is seen in everything He made,
But greater far the work He did, when on Him my sin was laid.

It took a miracle to put the stars in place;
It took a miracle to hang the world in space.
But when He saved my soul,
Cleansed and made me whole,
It took a miracle of love and grace.

Similar testimonies have been shared with me by people from many nations; differing cultures; and differing religious backgrounds. We read that after anointing Saul as king, Samuel said to him, *'Then the Spirit of the LORD will come upon you, and you will prophesy with them and be turned into another man'* (1 Samuel 10:6).

Once, when crossing a river in Georgetown, Guyana, I became engaged in a religious conversation with a Muslim man. I had learnt from past experiences to avoid getting into arguments over my faith, so instead I simply shared with this man how Christ had changed me. He did not have any answer to my testimony, so strong was the evidence!

During a tent mission in the Perth suburb of Victoria Park, a woman who was attending the crusade meetings came forward at the invitation time and confessed her faith in Christ. She told me that when she went home and told her husband that she was going to be baptized during the crusade, he angrily said to her, 'If you go ahead with this, I will come and disrupt the meeting'.

Naturally, we counselled her to put God first and trust that He would take care of everything. We also gathered a few members together to uphold her in special prayer and assured her that God's presence and power would be evident.

Despite her anxiety, the woman went ahead with her decision to be baptized. Her husband came and sat in the back row of the tent. However, he did not keep his promise to disrupt the meeting!

My message that night was centred on end-time prophecies. Later he told me that his intention was to do just as he had promised his wife, but as he sat in the back row, the Scriptures penetrated and gripped his heart. The next night he came back to the crusade to hear more! In fact, it was only a few nights later that he came forward to confess his faith in Christ and be baptized.

With a heart full of praise to God, I can share the fact that before the close of the four-week Crusade, 17 of this man's relatives and friends were also saved, all due to changes in his life and the testimony brought about by the power of the gospel.

Changed Lives in Kellerberrin

During another four week crusade in Kellerberrin, 70 souls accepted Christ and obeyed the gospel in baptism: Another 30 re-dedicated their lives to Christ.

One of those who confessed faith in Christ and submitted to baptism was an indigenous woman. I was told later by some people attending the crusade that they had seen her a few days earlier, lying drunk in the gutter in the near-by town of Doodlakine. After her baptism, this woman experienced an inner joy that was revealed distinctly on her face; as well as in her dramatically changed behaviour. God's saving grace—evidence for everyone to see!

During the course of this same crusade, two rough, disorderly shearers were also converted. The owner of the sheep station where they worked told me later that after their conversion, he watched them closely as they sheared the sheep. He said he felt compelled to ask the other workers, 'What has happened to these men'? He was astounded at the change in their work ethic, for both men were sober and they were no longer knocking the sheep around as they had done previously! Surely, this is another wonderful testimony to the transforming power of the gospel.

At some point in this crusade, a mother and daughter came forward to confess their faith in Christ. The next day, I went to visit them on their property, which was located just outside of town. I wanted to give them further teaching on the Biblical requirements for salvation! When I explained that repentance and faith were necessary to validate baptism, the daughter told me that she was ready to obey God's instruction. But the mother said, 'I want to be baptized, but I have *aquaphobia*' (a fear of being under water). She continued to share with me that her doctor had told her that she was never to put her head under water. To try to comfort and encourage her, I shared a few more verses of assurance from the Bible, as well as reading Acts 10:47[a], '*Can anyone forbid water, that these should not be baptized.*'

Before leaving their home, I made arrangements for the daughter to come into town for her baptism the following day. I then told the mother that if she decided to obey God in the waters of baptism, she should bring a towel and change of clothes with her. I also tried to help her decision by assuring her that I would have the water in the baptistery sufficiently heated to take away the chill and a stool for her to sit on as I lowered her gently back under the water.

The next day they both arrived at the aerosphere, and both were carrying a towel and a change of clothes. I asked the mother, 'Have you decided to be baptized'? Her joyous reply was, 'Yes, I have prayed and thought about what God says in the Bible and I have decided that it would be far better to die obeying God than to live in disobedience to Him'. I baptized both mother and daughter that day, without any physical effect on the mother, and two precious souls 'went on their way rejoicing'!

My Elderly Mother Obeys the Gospel

Closer to home and unknown to me until just before she went home to glory, my mother also suffered from aquaphobia. When I reflected on this newfound fact, I realized that I could not remember my mother ever going swimming. As I was growing up, I gave no thought to this, just assuming swimming was something she didn't like to do. My mother was a beautiful woman, a religious church-going woman, but she had not confessed Christ as her personal Saviour, or obeyed the gospel in baptism.

One night in 2004, when visiting my mother in the aged care home in Moree where she was residing, I was sharing with her about the conversion of the Ethiopian treasurer from Acts Chapter

Eight. As I read his confession, she stopped me and said, 'Doug, I believe that Jesus Christ is the Son of God'! This was the first time that I had ever heard my mother speak the name of Jesus Christ!

Upon hearing her words, and (as the saying goes), after 'picking myself up from the floor', I replied, 'Then there is nothing stopping you from being baptized'. Her baptism took place the following day, just a few months before her 96th birthday!

Even at her great age, her mind was still as 'bright as a button'. On my next visit to the home, a resident met me as I was walking down the hallway to my mother's room. She stopped me and asked, 'What has happened to your mother'?

I asked, 'Why'?

The woman replied, 'Because, your mother has come out of her shell! She has become the life of the party'.

What a dramatic change had taken place, because before her conversion my mother had always been withdrawn and shy.

Later, I was told that after her conversion my mother read her Bible every day, and on Sundays she read nothing but the Bible.

I would hope to persuade you with the fact that if God can do this for a 95-year-old woman, then it's not too late for anyone to give their life to Him. But, surely how much better to obey the gospel in one's youth, in order to give the whole of one's life in service to God!

Testimonies from India

In India, I have heard many converts come up from the waters of baptism saying, 'We love your Jesus! No one else has ever died for us so that our sins would be forgiven'.

At one village where I was preaching, a young man came walking toward the well where we were conducting the baptisms. His mother was calling out to him from their house, 'Son, don't leave our gods'! As he kept walking towards the well to obey the Lord, he shouted back, 'What have our gods ever done for us? Jesus Christ died for us'.

On yet another occasion in India, I was preaching and baptizing continually over a period of 17 days. During that time, my speaking schedule was very demanding and on average I preached three times a day. Towards the last day of my visit, having risen early to travel out to a village to preach, I was feeling very weary. We had started out early with the intention of catching the workers before they went out into the fields for the day's work. However, because we arrived later than planned, when we got there we only found some women, some invalids and some old people in the village.

Sitting down with the group, I asked them what it was that they needed more than anything else. I was expecting them to name one of the five basic physical needs of life. But one elderly man's response moved me to action, for he called out, 'HEAVEN'! As weary as I was, I immediately stood and preached the gospel and taught those present how to inherit the promise of eternal life. That day several precious souls were ushered into the kingdom of God.

Never Too Late!

On an earlier evangelistic trip to Ilford, London, I was accompanied by our dear friends Richard and Shirley Pearce. They led the singing and presented gospel items for the meetings, as well as helping me with the daily evangelistic visits!

After the message that night, an elderly woman came forward to confess her faith in Christ. We talked to her about her need to repent and be baptized. She replied, 'Yes, I will! I have missed two previous opportunities in my life to obey Christ and now that I am ninety, I am not going to miss out again'!

A Life Worth Living

When I reflect on my own conversion, I remember saying to myself, 'Now I am living'! I truly believe that before accepting Christ's call on my life, I had only been 'existing'! I simply lived for the next bout of pleasure or sport event.

After my conversion, I was living to serve God. For the first time in my life I knew where I had come from, why I was here and where I was going! I do truly grieve for those who are still walking in darkness, when they could be walking in the marvellous light of God, simply by trusting Christ for salvation and obeying the gospel.

A favourite chorus of mine sums up the testimonies that have been shared in this book. The words written by William and Gloria Gaither say:

Something beautiful, something good,
All my confusion He understood,
All I had to offer Him was brokenness and strife,
But He made something beautiful of my life.

'Jesus answered and said to him, "Most assuredly, I say to you, unless one is born again, he cannot see the kingdom of God." Nicodemus said to Him, "How can a man be born when he is old? Can he enter a second time into his mother's womb and be born?" Jesus answered, "Most assuredly, I say to you, unless one is born of water and the Spirit, he cannot enter the kingdom of God. That which is born of the flesh is flesh, and that which is born of the Spirit is spirit. Do not marvel that I said to you, 'You must be born again.'"

John 3:3-7.

A young Richard & Shirley serve God with their gift of music

Forever-friends and co-workers in evangelism—both in Australia and internationally

LOOKING GOD IN THE FACE

'Let us draw near with a true heart in full assurance of faith, having our hearts sprinkled from an evil conscience and our bodies washed with pure water.'

Hebrews 10:22

OVER THE CHRISTMAS NEW Year period of 1959-60 I had the wonderful opportunity to conduct a four-week crusade in a beach-side town some 223 kilometres south of Perth. This was my second of many tent crusades to follow, and it enabled me to daily fulfil my calling in proclaiming the message of salvation.

With John Timms as song leader, we set-out with youthful and eager hopes for a fruitful crusade (we were both in our early twenties). John also assisted me in visiting the people who were attending the meetings, as well as other contacts that we had been asked to call on.

We were praying for 40 souls to be won to Christ and for the church there to be fully established as a result of the crusade. Prior to the crusade, only two families were coming together at a house each Sunday to break bread.

The meetings were well attended every night and the Lord answered our prayers. By the closing night of the crusade 39 people had given their lives to Christ.

That night, following the closing meeting, we were enjoying sweet fellowship in the home of one of the original members, rejoicing, yet a little sad because we had not seen our anticipated 40 converts.

As we sat sharing and rejoicing, there was a knock at the back door. When the host opened the door he found a troubled young man standing there. As he entered the room I realized that this man's mother had been baptized during the crusade. He immediately asked us if he could be baptized as well. After sharing more fully with him, we returned to the tent and the portable baptistery in order to honour his wish to obey and follow Christ in the waters of baptism. What a wonderful encouraging God we serve!

As a result of this crusade, the church in the town of Busselton was fully established. Before very long, a building was erected with the generous gifts from new converts and the support of volunteer labour, a testimony to the souls who had been saved. The people whose lives had been changed were now overjoyed and desiring to use their gifts, both physically and financially, for God!

There were several other wonderful conversions during that four-week crusade. Decades later, it was my privilege to meet up with one of the converts, a glowing Christian, who was very active in a Perth church. Also, I was told that another family who came to the Lord at that time went on to be pioneers of another suburban church plant in Perth.

Another of the converts shared with me that before the crusade he and his wife had been on the verge of a marriage break up. He told me that they had reached a point where they were unable to agree on anything, even on whether to divorce or not.

Some months later, the wife also shared with me that after their conversion, their home had become a home of peace and life for them was now 'beautiful'! She added that for the first time since their marriage, she had been able to wash her husband's work overalls and not have to empty his pockets of filthy cigarette butts.

Several weeks after the close of the crusade, I was visiting some of the new converts, together with another evangelist, Jack Bond. Even as I write, after all these years, I still recall vividly one of those visits. The family in question lived a short distance out of town. The husband's name was Ken and he had been active in one of the local denominational churches. As we sat and engaged in conversation, I could not help smiling as a couple of chickens ran past us through the hallway.

The most memorable part of the visit for me was Ken's recounting of his conversion. He shared with us that on the night he responded to the invitation to make a personal commitment to Christ, as he came forward down the sawdust aisle he felt like he was 'walking on air'. What Ken shared next was so perfect, as he humbly voiced words that I will never forget: 'But, when I was baptized, as I came up out of the water, I felt that for the first time in my life I could look God in the face'.

As he spoke, the Scripture passage in 1 Peter 3:21[b] came to my mind and I opened my Bible and read, '*Baptism . . . the answer of a good conscience toward God.*'

> '*In the days of Noah, while the ark was being prepared, in which a few, that is, eight souls, were saved through water. There is also an antitype which now saves us—baptism (not the removal of the filth of the flesh, but the answer of a good conscience toward God), through the resurrection of Jesus Christ.*'
>
> **1 Peter 3:20[b]-21**

GOD'S CLOCK

'For He says: "In an acceptable time I have heard you, and in the day of salvation I have helped you.' Behold, now is the accepted time; behold, now is the day of salvation.'

2 Corinthians 6:2

IT HAS BEEN STATED that God is never late, rarely ahead, but unquestionably, always on time!

While ministering in America I placed a phone order for a new type of insect sonar repellent. I knew that I would have to leave the States before it could be delivered. However, the staff at Good News International said they would ship the package to my address in Australia as soon as it arrived at their office in Joplin, Missouri.

Because Nigeria was the next country on my evangelistic schedule, it was vitally important that I receive the repellent before I left Australia. While I was working in Nigeria on a previous visit I contracted a rare strain of malaria that had put me in hospital for 10 days, at times critically ill. Understandably, Nigerian mosquitoes were not my most welcome companions.

As I continued with planning my Nigerian trip, I made several attempts over many hours, to negotiate an earlier flight than the one available. My efforts were to no avail, and eventually my flight plans from Australia were delayed by one day.

About one hour before leaving for the International Airport in Brisbane, I received an email telling me that the package containing the sonar buzzer was waiting for me at the post office. Glory be to God! Right on time! Did God know that my flight would be delayed a day? Of course He knew! He knows everything and I do not doubt that He also had something to do with my delayed departure!

On another trip, this time to Lagos, Nigeria, my travel agent had informed me that on my arrival in Lagos, an ongoing ticket to East Africa could be purchased using local currency. Therefore, on arriving in Nigeria and acting on what I assumed was 'reliable' advice, I changed my Australian currency into local currency.

After having completed my ministry in Nigeria, on the day of my planned departure, I called at the office of Ethiopian Airlines, only to be told that I could not purchase my ticket with local currency. The ticket could only be purchased with US dollars, or with an American Express credit card. Neither of these two options were in my possession, nor was it possible to buy or change my local money into US dollars.

After unsuccessfully trying to purchase a ticket with several other airline companies located in the same city area, I knew that prayer was my only resource! If I could not board a plane that day, it would be another two or three days before I could get a flight to east Africa. I spoke once more to the man in charge at Ethiopian Airlines, but he was adamant that he was not able to grant my request. However, he did tell me that his supervisor had the 'last say'.

Wonderful! At last a man with authority, but, he was out of the office and was not expected back until closing time. My wait for his return seemed like forever!

My concern for having to travel at a later time was because my preaching schedules in Uganda had been advertised. They would need to be changed, and also, importantly, people would be inconvenienced by my late arrival.

Finally, the supervisor arrived back at the office and my opportunity to present my problem to him had arrived. He listened to my predicament courteously and then replied, 'What you were told is correct'!

At hearing his reply, my heart sank within me! I was about to thank him for his time, when he continued, 'But, if I was in your place and you were in mine, I would very much appreciate you doing something for me. So, I will break the rules and issue your ticket'. At last, the answer I needed, 'just in time'!

But following this victory, Satan was still lurking at the door!

I had now used all of my local money paying for my air ticket and I did not have sufficient left to get a taxi to the airport. Thankfully, the company realized my dilemma and assigned an employee to take me to where I could catch a bus. I was told that my guide would be waiting for me at the door! I walked out the front door, put my suitcase over my shoulder and started following a man standing outside the office, who, by his body language, appeared to be waiting for me.

However, you can imagine my dismay to discover that this man was not the employee of the airline company, but a criminal who was leading me down a street to rob me—or worse! Thankfully, before I had walked very far the real employee found out what had happened, and came running, shouting loudly, to rescue me. How good is our God!

I arrived at the airport just in time to catch my flight. My body may have sat on a seat in the plane that day, but my spirit was soaring on eagles' wings, praising God for His providential care.

God's perfect timing was again demonstrated during one of my early evangelistic tours to Nigeria. I was asked to visit a preacher in Ilorin, the state capital of Kwara in North central Nigeria. The only information I had been given to locate the man was a post office box number.

After travelling many hours by mini-bus, I finally arrived at my destination on Saturday afternoon. But, of course, the post office was now closed! What could God's servant do but wait and pray? As I sat praying, seeking His guidance on what to do next, a vehicle drove into the back yard of the building where I was sitting.

I was soon engaged in conversation with the driver! After finding out that he was an employee of the Post Office, I told him my predicament. The man then proceeded to open the back door of the Post Office and took me inside. He looked up the box number and found the address of the person I was asked to visit.

Before getting directions from this man and heading off, he informed me that it was very unusual for him to come to work after closing time. On this occasion a very specific reason had brought him back and whilst he did not share this with me, I think you know the real reason!

On another occasion in Nigeria, thieves stole my wallet from my pocket. One could be forgiven for asking God, 'Where were your protecting angels'? After filing a report at the police station and managing to get out of their office without paying a bribe, my next stop was the courthouse.

It was a well-known fact that no one ever left those 'halls of justice' without paying an 'enticement' to the corrupt officials. The thought of having to hand over my money for a bribe has always gone against my values. So, I proceeded to inform the chief official, in the presence of several staff members, what my beliefs were and why I was in their country. The official rather condescendingly said, 'Oh, so you are a preacher, are you'?

As I had done on similar occasions, my reply to him was, 'Yes, would you like me to prove it'?

When he answered in the affirmative, the gospel message proceeded out of my mouth as a witness to everyone present.

Was it worth losing my material possessions that day? The robbery placed me where I was able to tell others how to prepare for eternity! Just maybe, my angel was directed to allow the pick-pocket to take my wallet, so that I could fulfil the purpose that God had planned for me that day!

The Holy Spirit reminds us that we are to, *'Preach the word! Be ready in season and out of season. Convince, rebuke, exhort, with all longsuffering and teaching'* (2 Timothy 4:2).

On reading the events shared in this book, it may be a good time to ponder the following Scriptures that remind us of the time we have to get right with God. The Lord has given us all the same amount of time—24 hours in a day. We need to use that time in helping snatch sinners from the 'jaws of hell':

'And on some have compassion, making a distinction; but others save with fear, pulling them out of the fire, hating even the garment defiled by the flesh' (Jude 1:22-23).

'For the time has come for judgment to begin at the house of God; and if it begins with us first, what will be the end of those who do not obey the gospel of God? Now "If the righteous one is scarcely saved, where will the ungodly and sinner appear?"' (1 Peter 4:17-18).

Peter declared to the crowds in Jerusalem, *'Be saved from this perverse generation'* (Acts 2:40[b]). This reminds me of the words in Hosea 10:12, *'Sow for yourselves righteousness; reap in mercy; break up your fallow ground, for it is time to seek the LORD, till He comes and rains righteousness on you.'*

> *'Then they will call on me, but I will not answer; they will seek me diligently, but they will not find me.'*
> **Proverbs 1:28**

TO GO WHERE NO ONE HAS GONE—FOR CHRIST!

'He who did not spare His own Son, but delivered Him up for us all, how shall He not with Him also freely give us all things?'
Romans 8:32

MY ENTIRE ADULT LIFE has been committed to serving God. That service has presented me with many challenging adventures which have had eternal consequences! In all that I have set out to accomplish, my desire has been, and still is, to bring glory to God and to win lost souls to Christ. The results are not always as I intend, expect or even hope for, but my committed service to Him is my life-long goal.

Sometimes people have asked me how I have been able to prioritize the needs of my family and still be fully committed to the work of an itinerant preacher. My answer to that question has always been that I have never seen my family; my time of rest and relaxation; or my involvement with sport; as competing interests in my life!

Instead of placing my priorities like rungs on a ladder, I have always seen my life's commitments and activities as a circle, with God in the centre.

If I am relaxing or playing a game of golf, it is to get my mind and body in good shape so God can use me more completely. Now I know that some will say that such a statement is just an excuse to justify myself in fulfilling the desires of the flesh. Maybe they are right, but for me, it has always been a valid and practical way of handling my ministry, my family and my personal commitments!

Jesus was unmistakably clear when He declared, '*My mother and My brothers are these who hear the word of God and do it*' (Luke 8:21[b]). Again, we read in Luke 9:60 that Jesus plainly stated where our priorities should lie: '*Jesus said to him, "Let the dead bury their own dead, but you go and preach the kingdom of God."*'

To be a follower of Christ, especially if one is a preacher, one must take these words very seriously! There are plenty of people who are spiritually dead in this world—and they can take care of the physical things of life. As Christians, if our motives are correct, we can still enjoy family, sport and the God-given pleasures of life, without sacrificing our time spent in serving God.

What About a Wife?

According to the teachings of the New Testament, as preachers, missionaries and evangelists, we are entitled to take a wife with us on our journeys: and this has been true for me on several occasions. But I have been called to many places where I believe it would not be wise to take a woman. The exception would be if she was called by God to go, and also, in my opinion, if she was a very resilient person, one who was able to deal with many daily challenging, primitive and sometimes harsh travelling and living conditions.

A cross-cultural international evangelist has to be prepared to face hardships. These adversities come in many forms including: pit toilets; uncomfortable beds; encounters with thieves and terrorists; walking and travelling on rough and sometimes flooded roads; embarrassing bouts of diarrhoea; unsafe accommodation; at times hazardous travel by boat and train; and lack of proper medical care—just to name some! Of course, these things all fade into insignificance when considering Christ's sacrifice and our eternal rewards.

Hence, I have always had to evaluate whether it would be wise for me to take my wife, considering the situations I often faced in overseas missionary work?

Paul declares in 2 Corinthians 4:8-9, '*We are hard-pressed on every side, yet not crushed; we are perplexed, but not in despair; persecuted, but not forsaken; struck down, but not destroyed.*'

While I am not able to compare in any way my few hardships with those of Paul, I can still voice his words, *'For I consider that the sufferings of this present time are not worthy to be compared with the glory which shall be revealed in us'* (Romans 8:18).

'But He said to them, "Let us go into the next towns that I may preach there also, because for this purpose I have come forth."'

Mark 1:38

1996—Students (Lairawn Christian Youth Camp) following their baptism, Myanmar

TOOLS OF THE TRADE

'Beloved, you do faithfully whatever you do for the brethren and for strangers, who have borne witness of your love before the church. If you send them forward on their journey in a manner worthy of God, you will do well because they went forth for His name's sake, taking nothing from the Gentiles.'

3 John 1:5-7

Electric Windows

A RELIABLE CAR IS a tool of trade for a preacher doing visitation ministry and especially for an itinerant evangelist.

My first car was a 1929 Chevrolet. It was purchased from a local farmer and I share-owned the vehicle with my brother Ken. The body and bonnet of the car had been built for a six-cylinder motor, but this particular model only had four-cylinders. Hence, when doing repairs one could actually stand inside the uncluttered engine compartment to do the work—try doing that today in our modern cars!

My second car, a 1948 Ford Prefect, which was purchased while I was in Bible College, was share-owned with a fellow student! To help support myself through College, on Saturdays I worked as a vendor in Artarmon, a prestigious northern suburb of Sydney, selling ice cream from the vehicle's boot.

My third car was an unexpected blessing from the mightily-used evangelist, the late EC Hinrichsen. EC had visited the church where I was a student minister in Yennora, Sydney and observed the number of children that I was picking up to take to Sunday School. In those days one could cram a lot of people into one vehicle and still be within the law! The next day, EC took me to a second-hand car dealer and bought a 1936 Chevrolet. The bigger car was a wonderful assistance and such a great encouragement to me as a student minister.

Before leaving Sydney for my first ministry in Western Australia, I purchased a 1956 VW Beetle. Joyce and I packed a tea chest full of our meagre belongings and shipped them ahead to Narembeen.

The rest of our things were crammed into the VW. Every little space was used up, with the doormat and a cutlery set sitting on top of our luggage under the front bonnet—and lastly—a bassinet with our baby son Mark placed on top of everything else on the back seat.

Our first planned stop on the trip was in Adelaide, South Australia, where we picked up John Timms, who had decided to fly down from Sydney to join us. John found a spot for his suitcase in the back and squeezed into the front of the pint-sized VW, sharing one of the two bucket seats with Joyce. We drove like this to Port Pirie, where with some relief we boarded the train to take us and the car across the Nullarbor Plain to Kalgoorlie, Western Australia. We then resumed our awkward seating arrangement and drove the final leg down to Narembeen in the eastern wheat belt of the state. What an unforgettable journey—a total of 3,739 kilometres!

Some five years later, another ministry calling saw us returning to Queensland. By this time I had bought another VW and for this journey, instead of the train, I drove the 1,675 kilometres across the then dirt road of the Nullarbor Plain, from Norseman to Ceduna in South Australia. Sometime after completing this lengthy trip and arriving safely in Queensland, the car broke down.

Enter another blessing in the guise of Ian Boettcher of Boettcher Motors, Ipswich. Ian at that time was a butcher, but his love of cars and his backyard mechanical skills led him to a successful career in the motor vehicle and motor racing industry. Ian came to my rescue and repaired the car free of charge! Ian is still a supporter of my ministry and a faithful brother in Christ.

The VW was finally traded-in at the motor dealership of a generous Christian brother, John Buhse, of Laidley. John was well known by Queensland preachers, having helped a number of them purchase their vehicles at an affordable price. After taking my VW as a trade-in, John then returned it to me as a second car for my use in ministry. What wonderful friends and supporters have crossed our paths over the years!

A passing of time—and we now had four children, with a fifth on the way! A friend and member of the church in Warwick where we ministered offered to loan us money to purchase a bigger vehicle. He commented, 'With another child on the way you will need a station wagon to provide the extra room for a growing family'. With humble thanks, we agreed and bought the very popular 1964 EH Holden wagon that served us well for a good number of years.

It was only replaced when we were able to purchase a 1968 Holden Brougham belonging to Joyce's uncle, with money that she inherited from his estate. The children were delighted with the new car, especially with the electric windows.

Go Buy a Truck

With the move back from Western Australia to Victoria, the aerosphere, plus all the internal equipment and chairs were shipped there by train.

Later, we purchased a used furniture van to transport the aerosphere and equipment from one location to another. However, this left us without a car to get about and make ministry visits when we arrived at our destination.

A phone call was received one day from a Christian man (a brother of the late EC Hinrichsen) asking me to call in at his Real Estate office in Ipswich. When I arrived, I was greeted with the words, 'Doug, here's a cheque, I want you to go and buy a truck!' What an overwhelming joy filled my heart on hearing these words and it prompted my immediate praise to God for His provision, as a real need was met with this gift that day.

With the funds gifted, our ministry was soon the proud owner of a Ford F100! The vehicle was excellent in every way and almost a trouble-free utility for its time of service.

However, we still needed one final piece of equipment—a tandem trailer! We were so grateful when it was constructed and gifted to our ministry by a Christian brother from Geelong.

On delivery from Victoria, the tandem suspension on the trailer was put to the test when I accidentally backed over our toddler son Philip's chest. We thanked God that he came to no harm from this unfortunate accident: The outcome may have been very different if the trailer had been loaded with the aerosphere and equipment.

Another gift from the church in North Toowoomba saw the trailer fitted-out with a canopy. These generous gifts now meant that we had a truck and trailer for transportation of the aerosphere, as well as a reliable vehicle to use for visitation on arrival at a new crusade location.

With the arrival and fitting-out of the trailer, the van was no longer needed, and with the funds that we received from its sale I was able to fit-out the truck. The tray of the Ute was covered with a canopy and a bed was fitted in the back, as well as installing an additional 300 litre fuel tank, which was also located in the back of the vehicle. This effective set-up provided me with somewhere to sleep overnight when driving the long distances travelled in outback Queensland.

Eventually, after many kilometres travelled, the truck needed an engine overhaul. A dear brother from the Annerley church in Brisbane (who was a teacher of Mechanics at TAFE) stepped up and gave several hours of his free time to do an excellent job. His work served the vehicle well and it was reliable for the remainder of its time in God's service.

One unfortunate incident occurred during the lifetime of the trailer. It happened during a long trip from Queensland to Victoria. I took a nap in the back of the vehicle while two young co-workers took over the driving. On this occasion the trailer could have been packed more efficiently, because once on the road, it was obvious at speed that it tended to sway.

Then adversity struck! The trailer, still attached to the toe-bar, overturned!

Mercifully, the F100 never wavered or left the road. Thankfully, help soon arrived and the trailer was back on its wheels. After returning to Warwick to have it checked mechanically, we continued on our journey to Lower Templestowe for the next crusade.

I will not name the driver, but some will identify him from hearing him tell the story of how when he travelled with Doug Willis, the only stop for the day was to buy a loaf of sliced bread and a few bananas—all to be consumed whilst continuing the trip. Our travelling diet soon became known as, 'the evangelist's food'.

The End of an Era

After many years of service for crusades, the aerosphere finally deteriorated to such a point that it had very limited use.

At this time, I agreed to loan the aerosphere to a church group in Logan who wanted to use it as a trial before purchasing a larger aerosphere for their use. After picking up the aerosphere, the men were travelling interstate when they had an accident, with the trailer overturning and being badly damaged.

I did not know until after the event that it was wrongly assessed by the assessor and unceremoniously dumped. The assessor had mistakenly forwarded the insurance company a photo of a totally wrecked caravan, together with our claim details. Without contacting me, the insurance company authorised the wrecking yard to dump the 'van', somehow not understanding that it was in fact our trailer and equipment that was being dumped and not a caravan! After some interesting discussions back and forth, the company finally paid out on our claim.

By this time many things had changed in Australia and by the early 1980s tent crusades were no longer being supported as they had been in the past. The aerosphere had sadly reached its 'use by date'.

Another of the many vehicles that I owned over the years was a Mercedes Benz motor-home. It was the courtesy of an inheritance from my parents. The vehicle proved to be a beneficial means of giving Joyce (who suffered from rheumatoid arthritis) some precious times of relaxation, as we shared several enjoyable tours prior to her death from cancer in 2004. Rather reluctantly, in 2008 I made the decision to sell the vehicle due to the fact that my time spent overseas in ministry meant that the vehicle was not being used enough to warrant its upkeep.

My 'tools of trade' have been many and varied, mostly due to the unsolicited offers of loans; help with repairs; and the unexpected inheritances we were blessed with. However, each vehicle has played a big part in providing a means to conduct my travelling ministry, while clocking up around an estimated 2,500,000 kilometres.

God gave me a good sense of direction that was extremely helpful for the many kilometres travelled. More importantly, He gave me the understanding of my need to travel the 'highway of holiness' in order to minister effectively to others and look forward to eternal rewards.

We now drive a Hyundai i30, which we purchased one God-directed day in 2018. The car was four years old, but only had 5,000 kilometres on the clock—and at this stage of my life, I am more than happy for Loma to do the majority of the driving!

> 'And Abraham called the name of the place, The-LORD-Will-Provide; as it is said to this day, "In the Mount of the LORD it shall be provided."'
>
> **Genesis 22:14**

The Ford F100 and tandem trailer used to transport the aerosphere

FRESH AND FLOURISHING

'The righteous shall flourish like a palm tree, he shall grow like a cedar in Lebanon. Those who are planted in the house of the LORD shall flourish in the courts of our God. They shall still bear fruit in old age; they shall be fresh and flourishing, to declare that the LORD is upright; He is my rock, and there is no unrighteousness in Him.'

Psalm 92:12-15

IT COULD BE SAID by those of us who are getting old and grey-headed that it is time to retire! As yet, I have not found a verse in the Bible that says we should stop going into all the world preaching the gospel. Actually, Galatians 6:9 suggests just the very opposite, '*And let us not grow weary while doing good, for in due season we shall reap if we do not lose heart.*'

I doubt very much that many Christian ministers, evangelists or missionaries actually ever retire! Rather, they adjust to a different ministry, which I am, by God's grace, now striving to do.

In May 2018, together with a team of three others (Alan Horne, my Australian friend and fellow evangelist; and two of my grandsons, TJ and Jesse), I travelled to Papua New Guinea where I taught and mentored CEF students and others during the day and preached the gospel over a period of 11 consecutive nights.

Also, from 2012 to 2018, God enabled me to preach regularly at the Church of Christ in the Brisbane suburb of Zillmere.

My time is now spent: writing; mentoring preachers and our CEF students; encouraging support and gaining sponsors for evangelists in developing nations; and more importantly—reading God's Word and spending time in prayer for supporters, family and co-workers.

It may well be true that I am not fresh and flourishing on the outside, but the flame still burns brightly on the inside. Growing in grace and knowledge to become a better Christian and be more fitted for God's kingdom fills my time, with a bit of relaxation thrown in here and there.

You will note that every section of this book begins and ends with a Bible verse, so if you have been blessed by reading these events and experiences that occurred during my ministry, I pray it has instilled in you a greater appreciation and desire for God's Word.

I was once told that a dear brother from Ballarat stated, 'The problem with having Doug Willis staying in your home is that you get Bible for breakfast, dinner and tea'. I have to confess that his comment is mostly true!

While my experiences have been very real, they can never replace the Word of God: *'So then faith comes by hearing, and hearing by the Word of God'* (Romans 10:17).

God willing, this book will help answer my prayer, *'May the Lord of the harvest raise up and send forth labourers into the fields white unto harvest.'*

My life's journey has been, and still is, my testimony to God's faithfulness in His providence, protection and provision. He has been my constant companion over all the years of my life.

In the events shared in this book, you have read about the wonderful evidence of God's presence throughout my life's journey. This same God will walk with you in your daily life, if you are willing to launch out into the deep!

> *'Do not cast me off in the time of old age; do not forsake me when my strength fails. For my enemies speak against me; and those who lie in wait for my life take counsel together.'*
>
> **Psalm 71:9-10**

2008—teaching children English in China—with God's word

2011—Preacher-training Seminar, Orakkadu

2016—a new soul won for Christ (Calituban Island, Philippines)

2017—Teaching at the Cebu Christian College (Talamban, Cebu City, Philippines)

2018—The PNG Team (L to R) Doug, TJ, Jesse and Alan Horne

2018—Passing on the baton to grandson TJ!

2018—Creek baptisms at Bamaga, PNG

PERSONAL REFLECTIONS ON MY YEARS OF MINISTRY

'Then answered Amos, and said to Amaziah: "I was no prophet, neither was I a son of a prophet; but I was a sheep-breeder, and a tender of sycamore fruit"'.

Amos 7:14

A Passion Ignited

AT THE TIME OF God's call on my life, I was working on my father's dairy farm at Bexhill. While waiting on the milking machines to finish, I was musing over the possibility of getting into the pulpit of a nearby church to tell a friend and the congregation what they must do to be saved.

As if spoken audibly by a supernatural voice, three little words entered my mind: 'Why don't you'? So real was the voice, that I turned around and looked up to see who was speaking to me. When I saw no one, I realised that the words came from God.

Then, like Moses of old, I started making excuses!

My first response to this unseen voice was that there had never been any preachers in my family—my father was a cabinet-maker by trade—and a dairy-farmer.

My second excuse was that I wasn't a well-educated person.

But nothing I said to God that day could get those three little words out of my head: 'Why don't you'? So, my final response was, 'Lord, if this is what you want me to do, I will do it'.

My decision started a journey that led me to study for four years at Woolwich Bible College. There were many blessings during those years. I grew in my faith and knowledge of God's word—but I wanted more!

Bible College and Early Ministry in Australia

Without a doubt, my hometown preacher, the late Arnold C Caldicott, was instrumental in preparing me for Bible College and my future ministry.

Each Wednesday afternoon this enthusiastic and energetic preacher would take me with him to visit church members and contacts: I was 18 years old! We would make 10 or so positive, whirlwind visits, promoting the personal and congregational growth and life of the church.

Another of my mentors, mightily used evangelist the late EC Hinrichsen, told me that, 'Once you are able to get a person to commit to your specific request to them, it is time to leave'. As well, during my last year in Bible College, a beloved Sydney preacher, the late Ben Corlett, counselled me saying, 'Doug, once you say goodbye, go'!

Perhaps being mentored in this way was why I later earned the nickname from church members and friends of 'pop-in, drop-out Doug'.

Every Saturday night, I would join together with four or five other young men from the Lismore church, as 'AC' (a nickname Arnold was lovingly known by) taught us Bible lessons, and gave us instruction and experience in public speaking. Without his help and preparation, I am certain that I would not have lasted in Bible College for more than a few months.

As my confidence grew, I was soon invited to take part in the Sunday church meetings. As well, opportunities quickly arose for me to preach at the church in Bangalow, a small town 32 kilometres north of Lismore.

My first away from home sermon was titled *The Rich Young Ruler*, which I preached at the Church of Christ in Rosevale, Queensland. It was a borrowed sermon, one that I had read in a book (a collection of sermons by some of our Australian preachers) and I had memorised it practically word for word.

My entrance into Woolwich Bible College was mostly on faith. With very little money, I did not know where I was going to get the funds necessary to pay my way through the four-year course. I now know that this experience of trusting God completely for all my needs was preparing me for what lay ahead.

Preaching the gospel, both in churches and in open-air meetings, quickly became the focus and passion of my life. So it is not surprising that once in College, I became Secretary of the Woolwich Evangelistic Party (WEP). The group was made up of several students who sang and preached the gospel on the streets of Sydney suburbs, followed by gospel rallies in local churches.

My student ministry week was very full and consisted of: preaching at both the morning and evening Sunday meetings; teaching Sunday school; visiting contacts and church members on Monday; conducting a prayer and Bible study meeting on Wednesday night; besides the normal College classes and my studies Tuesday through Friday.

All this was great, but I was still convicted that I needed to accomplish more! At that time, I was mainly interested in the practical aspects of ministry and not so much in the academic field. My focus on academia came later!

To accomplish more, once a week I commenced an after-school happy hour for children in a nearby park. I purchased a piano accordion to help with the singing and a gifted accordionist from the Earlwood church taught me the basic chords that I needed in order to play the instrument. With practise, I quickly memorized several choruses for the children to sing and to learn about God's love.

Towards the end of my first year in College, I commenced what turned out to be a very fruitful student ministry at the church in Yennora. Many decisions were made for Christ during my two years of ministry and two men in particular went on to become preachers. One is still faithfully preaching the gospel and the other has since gone home to glory, after conducting God-blessed ministries in several churches.

My four years in Bible College were immensely enjoyable and beneficial. I believe I learnt more outside the classroom in discussions with fellow students than I ever did in class! In fact, during the countless lectures I attended, my mind was often given over to preparing sermon titles for a six-week series of gospel meetings, because my first love and my passion were bound up in tent missions (evangelistic crusades).

Whilst studying at Bible College two fellow-students, Maurie Pieper and Bruce Roberts, became close personal friends, as we grew together in our understanding and love for God's word. Together with our wives and families we have shared in many wonderful times of ministry and fellowship over the years and we remain close friends to this day.

First Tent Mission

It was in the beginning of my final year in College that I married Joyce and we commenced a much blessed life together in ministry.

Later that year I organised fellow students to help me in conducting a three-week crusade which we held in a tent at Wylie Park. Haydn Sargent was song leader, David Beavis was the pianist and Rex Ellis led the happy-hour for children in the afternoon. All three of these wonderful, godly men have now gone home to their eternal reward.

Following the crusade, a good friend and fellow preacher, the late Don Tonkin, negotiated a call for me to minister at the Church of Christ in Narembeen in Western Australia. When we arrived, we immediately commenced regular Sunday night gospel meetings.

During my second year in ministry at the church I received an invitation to conduct a crusade in the chapel in Merredin.

Then, at the end of 1959 I was asked to take the place of Jack Bond (who was the state evangelist for Western Australia), to conduct a tent mission at Busselton. I agreed to run the mission on the condition that John Timms could join me as song leader. Many lives were changed as a result of that mission.

Some years after, during a crusade I was conducting in Cardiff, New South Wales, the young preacher at the church asked, 'Do you remember me'? When I replied, 'No', he told me his story. 'I was one of the boys who got caught throwing stones on top of the tent in Busselton. The men on security duties made me go inside and sit and listen to your message. That night changed the direction of my life'.

After the Busselton crusade another tent mission soon followed in the Perth suburb of Victoria Park. Through the preaching of the gospel, God again touched and transformed many lives.

One woman, who had been raised in a Roman Catholic orphanage, shared her story with me. She recounted, 'The nuns forced us girls to go to confession every day: Because we could not think of anything to confess, we just made up stories and lied to the priest.'

Her words remind me of the Bible phrase, *'Having a form of godliness but denying its power.'* This woman came, listened, believed and obeyed the gospel, which is indeed God's power unto salvation!

Yet—still I was not satisfied!

I was (and still am), always praying and striving for more souls to be won for Christ. I longed to become more effective as an evangelist.

A Challenge Accepted

In 1962, I was being convicted of the need to continue my ministry on a faith-basis! After spending much time in prayer with Joyce, a decision was made to ask the church in Turlock, California, who was paying me a monthly salary, to stop their regular support. The church was informed that any gifts they were led to send from time to time would be appreciated. However, no further funds were given, until many years later! On reflection, I realize that I probably did not clearly explain to the church the purpose behind my decision. My thoughts at the time were that if I was going to preach and ask people to put their faith in Christ, then I should demonstrate my faith by trusting God to supply all my needs.

Accounts by earlier faith missionaries, such as Leonard and Retta Long, of the Australian Inland Mission, deeply influenced my decision. As well, George Müller's orphanage in Bristol, England, unquestionably demonstrated God's faithful provision for His servants. George Müller trusted God to place in people's hearts the need to send him the funds that he required to run the orphanage.

One incident that Müller shared in his book (*The Life of Trust*) occurred when the Bristol orphanage had run out of all food and money. However, that day Müller had the boys sit down at the meal table while he gave thanks for the food—food that was nowhere to be seen! Just as he was praying, a baker's cart came around the corner outside the orphanage, over-turned and spilt its load of freshly baked bread. Shortly after, the driver came through the door of the orphanage and asked if the Home could use the bread! They praised God for answered prayer and many hungry mouths were filled that day!

Many other missionaries at the time also practised faith-based support, not telling anyone except God, of their needs. These accounts of God's intervention and provision galvanized my resolve.

My decision to follow such examples was not taken lightly, as these events in the lives of faith-missionaries were from a past generation. So, how would a more sophisticated and modernised church in a more financially stable society respond? These thoughts were considered carefully and prayerfully and I admit, perhaps a little timidly! After all, does God not provide His servants with salaries on a faith basis? Yes, He does! But, there is a big differ-ence between a regular promised income and an irregular non-committed income.

Over the years, for income-tax purposes, I kept a record of the gifts that I received and that ledger is still in my possession. On adding up the monthly gifts I received, it can be seen that the total comes to about half the average wage at that time. However, God always provided through the many 'hand-me-downs' for the children and the food items that were graciously donated. These 'blessings', often left on our doorstep from an unknown source, supplemented the financial support we received.

Doors Open Internationally

In 1972 my overseas ministry—Worldwide Evangelistic Ministries (WEM) was born. Having conducted numerous crusades in every state of Australia over the previous two decades, I was called and convicted of the need to extend my ministry to overseas nations.

This new leading to start international work began with a three-month tour of Zimbabwe (formerly Southern Rhodesia). I worked as an associate evangelist with Reggie Thomas, who at that time was working with Revival Fires. During that mission tour in Zimbabwe the team was accompanied by the American vocalists, Janice & Faye Rostvit (*The Rostvit Twins*), who have a world-wide gospel music ministry. This initial ministry with the 'The Twins' was the beginning of many fruitful and happy tours together in several countries of the world, including Australia.

Ministry to India

My 40 years of ministry to India commenced in 1974. It was soon afterwards, during my second trip to India that God laid on my heart the concept of a ministry made up of Indian village evange-listic outreach teams. Over the next few years, those involved in this evangelistic outreach grew to three teams, totalling 18 preachers, all supported from Australia.

In 1981 the supervision and responsibility of this work was handed over to my good friend John Timms, who directed the Board of *Indian Village Evangelism* (IVE), based in Western Australia.

A few years later, I commenced a similar evangelistic outreach work in India under the name of SEEDS, with T John Samuel as Director. As it became more difficult to get sufficient sponsors from Australia, I approached Reggie Thomas and asked if WFOE could assist with raising support. I am thankful to God that Reggie took up my challenge and has co-worked with me in this ministry.

In the past 46 years, my overseas ministry has taken me to 40 nations, travelling to several of them on numerous occasions, preaching the gospel, conducting preacher-training seminars, speaking at conventions and lecturing in Bible Colleges.

In the year 2000, as a valuable tool to build up my teaching ministry, I accepted an appointment as the Dean for the South Pacific region and Overseas Branch Coordinator for CEF, the American-based Bible College (by distance education).

Lifelong Ban

The Indian government recently placed a lifelong ban on my entry into the country: Because over so many years I have preached the gospel and many nationals have been converted to Jesus Christ.

The ban led me to a decision to author and distribute training manuals to assist preachers with their ongoing learning and deeper understanding of New Testament teaching. Of particular assistance to national workers, my first book *Preparing to Become an Evangelist* and *Doing the Work of an Evangelist (Two in One)*, has been well received and is being used in Bible Colleges in India and Africa.

A second manual, *The Busy Man's Bible* and *The Cream of God's Word (Two in One)*, has since been published. Both books are now being distributed amongst my ministry contacts around the world and has provided me with another avenue to continue to deliver teaching and mentoring to my co-workers in foreign lands.

From Lowly Cow Bails to a King's Court

Being in the presence of this king took place during my last mission to Nigeria.

The crusade organizers for my 2013 ministry tour had included in my itinerary the privileged opportunity to preach in the court-yard of the King of the region where my co-workers and I were evangelizing. A large crowd had gathered and at the close of my message, the Queen, several chiefs, and many others from the gathering came forward to receive Christ as their Lord and Saviour.

The following day I was summonsed to a private audience with the King and Queen. What a privilege God provided, as a further opportunity opened for me to share the gospel. Before I left his court, the King assured me that when I returned, he would call his entire Kingdom to come and hear me preach!

I now lament that I will not be able to fulfil the King's invitation. I pray that a younger evangelist will be able to go and continue the work that God started in this King's heart and Kingdom.

Standing for The Faith

I am fully committed to 'the faith once for all delivered to the saints.' I believe without hesitation, that we are to do all that we can to reproduce the New Testament church, to the glory of God and the salvation of lost sinners. While God gives me health, strength and the means to proclaim the message of salvation, I am prepared and willing to serve Him in this way.

Having read the incredible experiences shared in this book, I trust you will make up your own mind about God's providence, but please remember to give God the glory and fully commit your all to

Him. It is only through God's calling on my life and His protection and provision that I have been enabled to do the things that I have accomplished.

So often I give praise and thanks to God that He counted me faithful, that He called me into ministry, and that He made me sufficient as a minister of the New Covenant.

God's Ongoing Plan and Purpose for My Life

In December 2004 my wife was called home to glory. Joyce had sacrificially given me her faithful and unwavering support through countless experiences, in good times, as well as through times of hardship and testing. She will always be remembered as a much-loved and dedicated minister's wife, as well as a loving and caring mother and a true friend to many.

After her death, I lost myself in ministry, spending an extended time working internationally; including visiting the Tsunami ravaged Andaman Islands to deliver aid and assistance.

But God had another plan and purpose for my life!

In November 2006 I married Loma Graydon, a widow from my home church in Lismore. Loma and her husband, Eric, had supported my ministry over the years, both prayerfully and financially. I had always known Loma as a woman of prayer, who sacrificially gave of herself in many ways: within the church; to her family and friends; and to the community.

Loma and her daughter Cathy Mooney have both been awarded The Order of the Medal of Australia (OAM), conferred by Queen Elizabeth II, for services worthy of particular recognition. The acknowledgement was for their work with the Leukaemia Foundation.

In September 1998, with Cathy at the helm steering the event, the Graydon/Mooney families held a fundraiser in the centre court of the Lismore Shopping Square. Their event raised A$80,000 and became the launching pad for *The World's Greatest Shave*. The event has grown to become one of Australia's biggest annual fund-raising events, raising in excess of A\$200,000,000 since its humble inception.

I share the following passage of Scripture in loving memory of my wife Joyce and in gratitude for the blessings that Loma now brings to my life and ministry.

> *'Who can find a virtuous wife? For her worth is far above rubies. The heart of her husband safely trusts her; so he will have no lack of gain. She does him good and not evil all the days of her life . . . Strength and honour are her clothing; she shall rejoice in time to come. She opens her mouth with wisdom, and on her tongue is the law of kindness. She watches over the ways of her household, and does not eat the bread of idleness. Her children rise up and call her blessed; her husband also, and he praises her: "Many daughters have done well, but you excel them all." Charm is deceitful and beauty is passing, but a woman who fears the LORD, she shall be praised."*
>
> **Proverbs 31:10-30**

Joyce

2006—Loma

Circa 1970s—The Church of Christ chapel, Lismore

1953—Saturday night Preacher Training Class with Arnold C Caldicott
Back Row (L to R) Trevor Taber, Stan McDonald, Jeff Davis
Front Row (L to R) George Davis, A C Caldicott, Doug Willis

1957—Wiley Park Tent Mission, Sydney

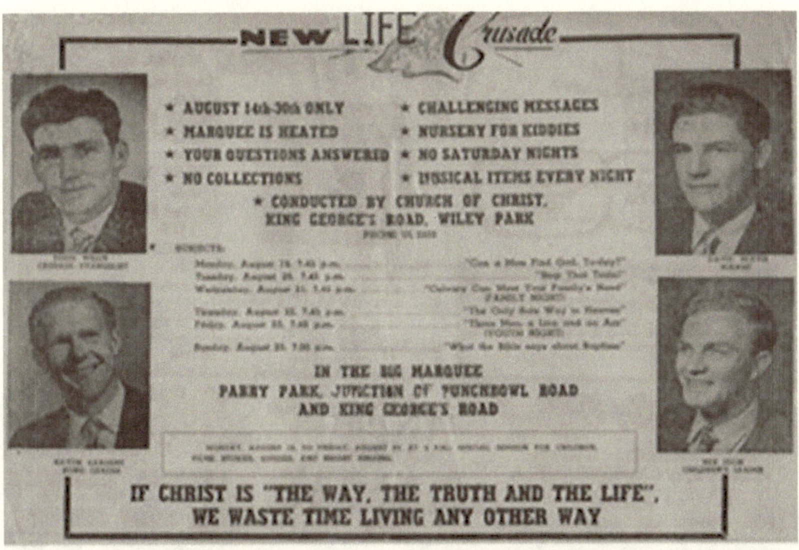

1957—Wiley Park Tent Mission with Woolwich Bible College Students:
Hayden Sargent, David Beavis and Rex Ellis

CEF South Pacific Office, Bribie Island (circa 2000)

*Guy Humphreys Founder of CEF (Head
Office in Coolidge, Arizona, USA)*

2005—Dr Doug—Associate Professor (ETS)

2007—Doug with the late Guy Humphreys (Cincinnati, USA)

2015—Doug with lifelong friends Bruce Roberts (left) and Maurie Pieper (centre) all graduates of Woolwich Bible College

AFTERWORD

'And Jesus came and spoke to them, saying, "All authority has been given to Me in heaven and on earth. Go therefore and make disciples of all the nations, baptizing them in the name of the Father and of the Son and of the Holy Spirit, teaching them to observe all things that I have commanded you; and lo, I am with you always, even to the end of the age."' Amen.

Matthew 28:18-20

The Results of a God-given Commission

AFTER READING THE ACCOUNTS of God's faithfulness shared in this book, it is my prayer some will heed the call and respond to God's great commission: and go into all the world preaching the gospel.

As a soul-winning evangelist; missionary and preacher, I ponder so often on the words of Jeremiah who wrote, *'Then I said, "I will not make mention of Him, nor speak any more in His name." But His word was in my heart like a burning fire shut up in my bones; I was weary of holding it back, and I could not'* (Jeremiah 20:9).

There are countless other Scriptures that have also been a challenge and encouragement to me and I share some of them with the hope and prayer that they will touch some young man's heart:

'For I am full of words; the spirit within me compels me. Indeed my belly is like wine that has no vent; it is ready to burst like new wineskins' (Job 32:18-19).

'What then shall I do when God rises up? And when He calls me to account, what shall I answer Him?' (Job 31:14—LITV).

'Also I heard the voice of the Lord, saying: "Whom shall I send, and who will go for Us?" Then I said, "Here am I! Send me." And He said, "Go and tell this people."' (Isaiah 6:8-9[a]).

'Those from among you shall build the old waste places; you shall raise up the foundations of many generations; and you shall be called the Repairer of the Breach, the Restorer of Streets to Dwell In' (Isaiah 58:12).

And, yes, I feel like Paul who wrote:

'For if I preach the gospel, I have nothing to boast of, for necessity is laid upon me; yes, woe is me if I do not preach the gospel!' (1 Corinthians 9:16).

'And I thank Christ Jesus our Lord who has enabled me, because He counted me faithful, putting me into the ministry' (1 Timothy 1:12).

'For the love of Christ compels us, because we judge thus: That if One died for all, then all died' (2 Corinthians 5:14).

I liken my own calling and commission to that of Ezekiel and Jeremiah, who heard God's commission loud and clear:

'And He said to me: "Son of man, I am sending you to the children of Israel, to a rebellious nation that has rebelled against Me; they and their fathers have transgressed against Me to this very day. For they are impudent and stubborn children. I am sending you to them, and you shall say to them, "Thus says the Lord GOD." As for them, whether they hear or whether they refuse—for they are a rebellious house—yet they will know that a prophet has been among them. And you, son of man, do not be afraid of them nor be afraid of their words, though briers and thorns are with you and you dwell among scorpions; do not be afraid of their words or dismayed by their looks, though they are a rebellious house. You shall speak My words to them, whether they hear or whether they refuse, for they are rebellious' (Ezekiel 2:3-7).

'Then the word of the LORD came to me, saying: "Before I formed you in the womb I knew you; before you were born I sanctified you; I ordained you a prophet to the nations." Then said I: "Ah, Lord GOD! Behold, I cannot speak, for I am a youth." But the LORD said to me: "Do not say, 'I am a youth,' for you shall go to all to whom I send you, and whatever I command you, you shall speak. Do not be afraid of their faces, for I am with you to deliver you," says the LORD. Then the LORD put forth His hand and touched my mouth, and the LORD said to me: "Behold, I have put My words in your mouth. See, I have this day set you over the nations and over the kingdoms, to root out and to pull down, to destroy and to throw down, to build and to plant"' (Jeremiah 1:4-10).

Additional Scriptures remind me of Paul's words—words that were of great encouragement to me when I was a young preacher, and I pray will speak to you if you are considering serving God in the same way I have.

'Let no one despise your youth, but be an example to the believers, in word, in conduct, in love, in spirit, in faith, in purity' (1 Timothy 4:12).

To belong to such a distinguished band of evangelists is my honour and I seek to always heed the words that record the purpose of Christ's ministry and commission:

'But He said to them, "I must preach the kingdom of God to the other cities also, because for this purpose I have been sent"' (Luke 4:43).

'So Jesus said to them again, "Peace to you! As the Father has sent Me, I also send you"' (John 20:21).

Philip was known as an evangelist because, just like Jesus, he went out to evangelize in 'all the other cities'. We read in Acts 8:40, 'But Philip was found at Azotus. And passing through, he preached in all the cities till he came to Caesarea.'

Our Lord spoke a parable relative to my ministry, which Luke recorded in 17:7-10:

'And which of you, having a servant ploughing or tending sheep, will say to him when he has come in from the field, "Come at once and sit down to eat?" But will he not rather say to him, "Prepare something for my supper, and gird yourself and serve me till I have eaten and drunk, and afterwards you will eat and drink?" Does he thank that servant because he did the things that were commanded him? I think not. So likewise you, when you have done all those things which you are commanded, say, "We are unprofitable servants. We have done what was our duty to do."'

I have at times felt like the preacher who travelled with John Wesley. He was standing on his box in the open air, preaching his heart out. Passing by, some hooligans took delight in throwing stones at him. One struck the preacher on the head. He stopped speaking, got down from his box and wiped the blood from his face. He then stood back up on the box and said, 'Young men, I am willing to suffer for you, I am even willing to die for you, but I am not willing to go to heaven without first telling you the way to abundant happiness and eternal life.'

Throughout my life of ministry I have endeavoured to do my loving duty to my Lord who saved and redeemed me. I am now cleansed, sanctified, justified, reconciled and adopted into God's family! The Lord be magnified!

'Now the Lord came and stood and called as at other times, "Samuel! Samuel!" And Samuel answered, "Speak, for Your servant hears."'

1 Samuel 3:10

EPILOGUE

Things We Should all be Looking Forward to in Heaven

The following Scriptures are a real blessing to me as I reflect on eternity and I share them in the hope that you will also be blessed as you read:

'Surely goodness and mercy shall follow me all the days of my life; and I will dwell in the house of the LORD forever' (Psalm 23:6).

'You will show me the path of life; in Your presence is fullness of joy; at Your right hand are pleasures forevermore' (Psalm 16:11).

'As for me, I will see Your face in righteousness; I shall be satisfied when I awake in Your likeness' (Psalm 17:15).

'One thing I have desired of the LORD, that will I seek: that I may dwell in the house of the LORD all the days of my life, to behold the beauty of the LORD, and to inquire in His temple' (Psalm 27:4).

'His lord said to him, "Well done, good and faithful servant; you have been faithful over a few things, I will make you ruler over many things. Enter into the joy of your lord"' (Matthew 25:23).

'Blessed be the God and Father of our Lord Jesus Christ, who according to His abundant mercy has begotten us again to a living hope through the resurrection of Jesus Christ from the dead, to an inheritance

incorruptible and undefiled and that does not fade away, reserved in heaven for you' (1 Peter 1:3-4).

'Therefore, brethren, be even more diligent to make your call and election sure, for if you do these things you will never stumble; for so an entrance will be supplied to you abundantly into the everlasting kingdom of our Lord and Saviour Jesus Christ' (2 Peter 1:10-11).

'Now I saw a new heaven and a new earth, for the first heaven and the first earth had passed away. Also there was no more sea. Then I, John, saw the holy city, New Jerusalem, coming down out of heaven from God, prepared as a bride adorned for her husband. And I heard a loud voice from heaven saying, "Behold, the tabernacle of God is with men, and He will dwell with them, and they shall be His people. God Himself will be with them and be their God. And God will wipe away every tear from their eyes; there shall be no more death, nor sorrow, nor crying. There shall be no more pain, for the former things have passed away"' (Revelation 21:1-4).

'And he showed me a pure river of water of life, clear as crystal, proceeding from the throne of God and of the Lamb. In the middle of its street, and on either side of the river, was the tree of life, which bore twelve fruits, each tree yielding its fruit every month. The leaves of the tree were for the healing of the nations. And there shall be no more curse, but the throne of God and of the Lamb shall be in it, and His servants shall serve Him. They shall see His face, and His name shall be on their foreheads. There shall be no night there: They need no lamp nor light of the sun, for the Lord God gives them light. And they shall reign forever and ever' (Revelation 22:1-5).

'For I am hard-pressed between the two, having a desire to depart and be with Christ, which is far better.'

Philippians 1:23

RECOGNITIONS

'I am the LORD, that is My name; and My glory I will not give to another.'

Isaiah 42:8[a]

Below are several unsolicited written recognitions from friends, colleagues and co-workers attesting to God's blessing on Doug's devoted and sacrificial ministry over 60 years. More than 40 of those years have been focused on the international mission field, the fields, 'white unto harvest'!

I am looking forward to reading this book! I highly recommend it to your friends, co-workers and the whole public. What a dedicated life and evangelistic ministry you have had as an effective, but humble servant of Christ. Bob.

2019

Bob Vernon

Sherman Oaks (USA)

I am so thankful that TJ and Jesse got to go with you on this trip to PNG. That makes three of your grandsons now who have gone on mission tours with you. May the example you set in love, speech, and deed in sharing Christ never be forgotten! Anna.

2018

Anna Smiddy-Daniels

Wheatfield, Indiana (USA)

I am in awe of all you do for the Lord. Your focus has never wavered. You are a great example of what Christ called the 'single eye'. You have touched thousands of lives for the Lord on five (or six) continents! I salute you, Doug, and thank God for you. You touched my life and many others in Central California. Wayne.

2018

Dr Wayne Bigelow

California (USA)

Doug, I have been back from Africa for a month. The trip was an overwhelming success and completely exhausting. In Uganda, East Africa, we met your co-workers: Isaac Mugerwa; Johnmark Ighorodhe and Jehoshophat Kakooza. Johnmark is doing an incredible work in Nigeria. I want you to know that your name is much loved and respected among the brothers in Africa. You have done a good work there and it shows. Jeff.

2018

Jeffrey D Brown—Dean of the School

Christ's Evangelical Foundation

Saint Robert, Missouri (USA)

When I was a student in Morris Bible College at Madras in 1976 I met a stranger, a slim and fit Australian evangelist among the Americans whose name was Doug Willis. I believe there has been no other Australian evangelist in our time that has been able to meet so many people, preach the gospel and win more souls, and plant more churches around the world than you have. We praise God for your life as you have, since the 1970s, and still are, being a blessing to Indian churches. Paul.

2018

Paul Raghu

Evangelist, Tamil Nadu, India

Since more than 40 long years you have done your service in India for God's glory and won many hundreds of souls to the Lord Jesus Christ, and they are now added to the Lord's church. You selected us young evangelists from different areas, cultures and caste-backgrounds. You taught us about Jesus Christ and trained us to follow sound Bible doctrine. You visited India often; encouraged us; told our sponsors about our work and needs; collected funds and sent many thousands of dollars to various ministry groups.

Whenever you visited India you came with us to villages; stayed with us in the houses made of mud walls and thatched roofs; conducted many preacher seminars for us and for denominational preachers. You taught them New Testament doctrines and practices that were previously unknown to them; you preached in village mini-conventions; as well as big conventions where thousands gathered in our base compound.

You preached the gospel on many village street corners and ate very simple and humble food with us. We are so grateful to you always because of your efforts to support the poor evangelists of India. If your support and advice had not been available, my ministry would be no more! You are really a dedicated man of God, and Christ's truthful servant you can truly say, *'I have fought the*

good fight, I have finished the race, I have kept faith' (2 Timothy 4:7).
Timothy.

2017

The late MT Timothy

Director, Titus Teams

Orakkadu, Tamil Nadu, India

Doug, Let me share a story of 57 years ago. It happened after the first night that I attended the Yennora Church of Christ in Fairfield, Sydney, where a young red-haired Bible college student was preaching. At that time I was working at Cockatoo Island Naval Base, doing my final year of my shipwright apprenticeship. Getting off the ferry at Circular Quay, I was walking up George Street in Sydney to catch the train home and who should be walking just ahead of me but that same preacher whom I heard speaking on the previous Sunday.

Without him knowing, I got in behind him and walked in his footsteps for some distance. Perhaps that has been what I have been doing for the past 57 years. I praise God so often that you set the example for me to follow. John.

2017

John Timms

Evangelist

Perth, Western Australia

I recently had occasion to use your name in a Bible study. My Bible group is studying Ephesians and using a Max Lucado book. One of the questions in the 'reflection' section asked, 'Do you know anyone who exemplifies strong faith in action?' I told the participants about you and your trips to many countries to share about

Jesus. Thank you so much Doug for being that 'strong faith in action' person for me. Sandy.

2016

Sandy Jarrett
Kansas City (USA)

'But let him who glories glory in this, that he understands and knows Me.'

Jeremiah 9:24[a]

Keep Going Strong

Keep going strong, my sturdy friend;
There are still many things in this world to mend.
And I know you've the mind and the strength as well,
To continue God's battle 'gainst the powers of Hell.

So put on your armour and pick up your spear,
And prepare for battle in this brand New Year,
For the devil is still a real, sturdy foe,
Seeking and striving real sorrow to sow.

But you have the weapon most powerful of all:
In your hands, the Gospel can nations make fall.
So go out to battle with ne'er any doubt,
And your Gospel the devil will surely cast out.

And friends 'round the world will bless your name,
Calling on the Lord to strengthen your game,
And make you a winner in the war of all wars,
As you carry the battle to many strange shores.

So as you begin this New Year, aught six,
Take a good look at the things left to fix;
And put on your armour and pick up your spear
To go out and make this a victorious year.

And the Lord of all life will prosper you
In the things worthwhile in your clear view;
And you will find joy and peace as reward
For loyal service to your Lord given abroad.

Circa 2000

The late Guy Humphreys

Founder and President of Christ's Evangelical Foundation
Doug's much loved co-worker and brother in Christ

OTHER PUBLICATIONS BY THE AUTHOR

Manual

Preparing to Become an Evangelist and *Doing the Work of a New Testament Evangelist* (Two in One)

Topical Reference Manual

A Busy-Man's Bible and *The Cream of God's Word* (Two in One)

Gospel Tracts

Christian Music

Directions to the Father's House

Four Things the Devil Doesn't Want You to Know

Gender Equality

Great Stories of Conversions

Have you Been Converted?

How Important Is It to Belong?

How Many Baptisms are There?

How We Can Know the Truth?

Is Hearing and Believing Enough?

Is the Devil Using Music?

Is There a Hell?

Jesus Christ, Who is He?

Love and Hate

Obeying the Gospel

Objections to Baptism Answered

Once Saved — Always Saved?

Prayer: The Right and Wrong Ways to Pray

Should Christians Live Under Law?

The Apostle's Doctrine

The Case for Weekly Communion

The Gift of the Holy Spirit

The Holy Spirit and Laying on of Hands

The Hour of Power

The Multi-locational Church

The Name Above all Names

To Sin or Not to Sin

Unfulfilled Prophecies

Washed in the Blood

Who is the Holy Spirit?

Women Teachers

Worship

You Can be Certain of Salvation

**If you have enjoyed reading this book,
then help us get the word out!**

- Share a link to the book on social media
- Write a review on your blog
- Pick up another copy to share with someone
  you know needs a little 'faith-lift'
- Recommend this book for your church, book
  club, or home groups

For further information please contact the author
and share your thoughts at:
🖱 **wemcef@gmail.com**

Or write to:
✉ **Worldwide Evangelistic Ministries**
   PO Box 49
   WOODY POINT QLD 4019
   AUSTRALIA